The Lime Green Myste

The Lime Green

Rosa Schling

Mystery:

an oral history of the Centerprise co-operative

On the Record

For the people of Hackney, past and present.

In memory of Athaliah Durrant, Howard Mingham, Lotte and Siege Moos, Bridget O'Connor, Ann Taylor, Glenn Thompson, Vivian Usherwood, and the many other people who contributed their time, energy and ideas to Centerprise who are no longer with us.

First published by On the Record, 2017

On the Record
123 Paulet Road
London SE5 9HW

Copyright © On the Record, 2017

All rights reserved. No part of this book may be reprinted or reproduced or utilised in any form or by any electronic, mechanical, or other means, now known or hereafter invented, including photo-copying and recording, or in any information storage or retrieval system, without permission in writing from the publisher

British Library Cataloguing in Publication Data

A CIP catalogue record for this book is available from the British Library

ISBN 978-0-9927393-1-7

This book was designed, typeset and made into pages in Adobe InDesign by Peter Brawne, Matter, London. The text was set in the typefaces Rockwell (various weights), Egyptian 710 and Egyptienne Condensed Bold (headings). The book was printed and bound by L&S Printing, Worthing and London

This publication was published with financial support from the Heritage Lottery Fund

Cover images credits
Front, clockwise from top left:
Copyright © Doffy Weir, Sherlee Mitchell,
Brian Longman, Courtesy of London Borough of Hackney Archives.
Back, clockwise from top left:
Copyright © Hackney Photos, Sherlee Mitchell,
Alan Denney, Unknown.

on-the-record.org.uk

Contents

    Preface / 9

1:   **Making the idea real** / 15

2:   **In search of the people** / 23
      Schools, strikes and newspapers / 24
      On Dalston Lane / 31

3:   **Buildings have history** / 41
      On the frontline / 41
      Behind the shopfronts / 52
          The bookshop / 55
          The coffee bar / 63
      The basement / 71
          The 136 playgroup / 71
          Youth / 71
      The first floor / 79
          Offices and meeting rooms / 79
          The advice centre / 81
      Hackney Reading Centre / 89
      The publishing project / 103

4:   **An attempted jail break** / 123
      We not I / 125
      Just writing it down / 130
      We should be grateful / 134

5:   **The collective** / 143
      The only way to work / 143
      The collective ends / 155
      The closure / 158

6:   **Conclusion** / 161

Centerprise, c. 1992. Photograph courtesy of Tom Woodin.

Preface

When it opened in 1971 Centerprise was the only bookshop in Hackney, east London, then one of the most deprived parts of England. Centerprise's radical founders believed this was a deliberate omission by arbiters of culture like the large publishers and booksellers, who thought that working class people had no interest in, or need for, literature. Opening a bookshop was therefore a political act, meant to assert access to books for all as a "cultural right". The bookshop was swiftly complemented by a publishing project that "made public" the writing, poetry and life stories of hundreds of local people, selling many thousands of their books. It proved that not only did the people of Hackney read, they wrote too.

More than just a bookshop, Centerprise was once described as a "lime green mystery, trading ambiguously in an otherwise strictly commercial high street."[1] A coffee bar offered cheap teas, meals and a welcoming and sociable atmosphere. Behind the shopfronts the building housed youth projects and children's activities, cultural events and exhibitions, office facilities and meeting rooms, an advice centre, a playgroup, adult education classes, writers' and local history groups, a publishing project and a reading centre that taught adult students literacy. This combination of services provided within one place was meant to open doors to experiences that may otherwise have been out of reach, and it was hoped Centerprise would have a transformative impact on the lives it touched. Someone might come in for some advice and leave having been inspired to write a book, or at least having bought one.

Centerprise hoped to distinguish itself from charitable or philanthropic social work projects that may have provided similar services, but which seemed to reinforce divisions between the "do-gooders" who ran them and those who were "done to". In 1981, on its tenth anniversary, they wrote:

> **if there has been one constant theme in Centerprise's philosophy ... [it] has been the continuing attempt to break down the very fixed categories of people's roles which so many other established social forms and institutions have handed down to us: teacher/taught, writer/reader, producer/consumer, artist/audience, men's work/women's work, mental/manual.**[2]

This work was "permanently unfinished"[3], as Centerprise itself acknowledged, and always complicated by dynamics of class, gender and race. Differences between those who ran the project as workers or co-operative members and those who used the project as customers, writers and group members, were not, perhaps could not, be obliterated. Issues of representation, power and participation in the centre's work continued to be the subject

---

[1] Centerprise Trust Ltd, 'Centerprise Annual Report 1978', 1978, A Hackney Autobiography, Bishopsgate Institute.

[2] Centerprise Trust Ltd, 'Press Release: 10th Anniversary, 20 April 1981, Arts Council of Great Britain Archive.

[3] Centerprise Trust Ltd, 'Centerprise Annual Report 1978'.

of discussion, debate and challenge from within and without, evolving as Centerprise, and the world around it, changed.

Centerprise was part of a broader movement that sought to democratise culture in multiple arenas: youth work, education, people's history, community publishing. It was conceived of as a pre-figurative project, foreshadowing in its processes a more equal future society. One important way it tried to do this was through its collective management structure whereby the workers ran the centre, overseen by a larger co-operative of local people. This could only ever have been an imperfect attempt, the demands of the outside world intruded, and the collective itself was far from ideal. In 1984, a Centerprise worker described the idea of Centerprise being pre-figurative as seeming like "an absolute bloody joke" in the context of Thatcherite Britain, when everything hard fought for in the previous decade seemed about to be undone by cuts and closures.[4]

However, it is the attempt Centerprise made to put these radical ideas into practice, while providing a range of useful activities and services over several decades, that makes it especially interesting today. Throughout this book excerpts of interviews with those involved with the co-operative are used to provide insight into the fine detail of what worked and what didn't, the lessons learnt, in hindsight what would have been done differently and what those involved got out of it, to form a collectively sourced body of knowledge meant to inspire and inform those engaged in similar work today.

This book has been produced as part of the oral history project A Hackney Autobiography: Remembering Centerprise, run by On the Record and funded by the Heritage Lottery Fund. The project spent from December 2014 to December 2016 collecting an archive of documents, photographs and ephemera at the Bishopsgate Institute's library in east London, and recording interviews with over forty people: former workers, customers and local residents who remember Centerprise.[5]

There were many people we wanted to interview but couldn't get to or did not locate in time. Given the number of projects housed within Centerprise we would have needed more time to have collected a fully representative set of interviews. Interview quotes have been edited for brevity and clarity from verbatim transcripts in consultation with interviewees. They retain a sense of their origins as speech, not writing. Where possible, every effort has been made to discuss quotes with interviewees, and around fifty people, including most interviewees, have given feedback on drafts of this book.

As one interviewee remarked, and as applies elsewhere, every person involved thinks that the period of Centerprise they remember was the "real" Centerprise. One of the most significant ways in which it changed over the years was that by the early 1990s most of the people who worked at and used Centerprise were from ethnic minority communities, which was not the case in its first two decades. Judy Joseph, for instance, who used to visit Centerprise in the 1990s and 2000s remembered it as a black organisation. She

---

[4] Betsy Brewer, Interview with Betsy Brewer by Maggie Hewitt, 19 October 1984.

[5] Quotes from the oral history interviews recorded as part of A Hackney Autobiography: Remembering Centerprise and archived at Bishopsgate Institute. are attributed to the interviewee in the text but are not referenced separately.

recounts her surprise at the project's launch event when she "encountered visually" a crowd of mainly older white people "because my expectations were to find older, black people."

Centerprise was open from 1971 until 2012, but this book focuses its attention on its era of co-operative management, which came to an end in 1993. This partly reflects the material we have recorded, which is heavily weighted towards the earlier period.

Chapters 1 and 2 give a detailed account of how the idea of Centerprise arose, was "made real" and what the project did in its experimental first few years. The beginnings of Centerprise are set in the broader context of Hackney at the time, wider developments in education and the youth-led counter culture. Chapter 3 opens with Centerprise's move onto the "frontline" of Kingsland High Street, where it attracted a more diverse group of customers, experienced attacks by the far right and witnessed the funeral marches of those who had died in police custody. Behind the shopfronts the reader is taken on a tour of each floor and every project it housed. Chapter 4 explores issues of participation, power and representation that arose in various aspects of Centerprise's work: in the collective groupwork of "A People's Autobiography of Hackney", in the publishing work of the Hackney Reading Centre that raised debates about dialect and language and in the relationships between writers and editors, especially as they related to the representation of ethnic minority writers. Chapter 5 examines the workings of the collective in detail and gives an account of how it ended and, many years later, how Centerprise's closed. The conclusion discusses the impact of Centerprise on the people who worked at and used the building.

Acknowledgements

Thank you firstly to the people whose interviews make up this book: Oleander Agbetu, Toyin Agbetu, Liesbeth de Block, Pauline Brown, Anna Davin, Oliver Flavin, Margaret Gosley, Richard Gray, Bernadette Halpin, Maggie Hewitt, Rosie Ilett, Anthony Kendall, Ken Jacobs, Judy Joseph, Eva Lewin, Neil Littman, Chris O'Mahony, Claudia Manchanda, Ric Mann, Neil Martinson, Michael McMillan, Jean Milloy, Roger Mills, Gary Molloy, Manju Mukherjee, Wendy Pettifer, Nick Pollard, Janet Rees, Barbara Schulz, Irene Schwab, Robin Simpson, Judith Skinner, Dorothea Smartt, Jud Stone, Pauline Wiltshire, Larraine Worpole and Ken Worpole.

Thank you to all volunteers who conducted interviews, research and carried out numerous other tasks, the archive contributors and the steering group members who made the project A Hackney Autobiography: Remembering Centerprise happen, to our project partners, Bishopsgate Institute, and funders, Heritage Lottery Fund.

Interviews were conducted by a team of volunteers: Olivia Bellas, Charlie Clarke, Wallis Eates, Farhana Ghaffar, Richard Gray, Julia Gray, Ruth Geall, Maggie Hewitt, Judy Joseph, Bea Moyes, Mary Mullen, Sean Mullervy, Nell

The Lime Green Mystery

Twenty-fifth anniversary event at Centerprise on the past and future of radical and community publishing, 1996. Left to right: Glenn Thompson, Roger Mills, Margaret Busby and Ken Worpole. Copyright © Larraine Worpole.

Osborne and Beth Young, along with myself and Laura Mitchison.

Another group of volunteers carried out research: Daniele Alexandre, Charlie Berry, Liesbeth de Block, Elin Jones, Judy Joseph, Ruth Geall, Bea Moyes, Sean Mullervy, Sarah Okpokam, Dominic Simpson, Eva Turner and Richard Wright. Elin Jones's investigations into the Hoxton Café Project, the Centerprise collective and the Arts Council archive and Charlie Berry's detailed and insightful research into the history of working class social and political life in Hackney and the funding of Centerprise by Hackney Council especially informed this book.

Thank you to all the photographers, writers and artists who allowed us to use their work to illustrate this book, especially Hugh Boatswain, Alan Denney, Ruby Moran, Sherlee Mitchell, Ingrid Pollard, Anna Sherwin and Doffy Weir. Thanks also to the staff at Hackney Archives, Bishopsgate Institute (especially Stefan Dickers) and the excellent Radical History of Hackney website, all of whom helped locate vital images and information.

This book developed in conversation with almost all the interviewees and many others with a connection to, or interest in, Centerprise. In all over fifty people took the time to answer my questions and feed in their thoughts.

Thank you especially to Liesbeth de Block and Ken Worpole, who gave me their detailed responses to a full draft. Apart from many of the interviewees, who generously gave me their feedback and responded to my interminable queries, I'd like to thank especially Toyin Agbetu, Kelly Bornshlegel, Guy Farrar, Margaret Gosley, Bernadette Halpin, Maggie Hewitt, Sheila Hildreth (Greenwood), Rosie Ilett, Michelle Johansen, Judy Joseph, Anthony Kendall, Jane Laporte, Michael McMillan, Chris O'Mahony, Claudia Manchanda, Neil Martinson, Manju Mukherjee, Hilary Povey, Janet Rees, Irene Schwab, Robin Simpson, Jud Stone, Pauline Wiltshire and Larraine Worpole for their thoughts and assistance.

A Hackney Autobiography was coordinated by both Laura Mitchison and myself. This book results from our collaborative work, and owes much to Laura Mitchison's editing and perceptive mind. Its faults are entirely my own.

Claire Garner meticulously copy-edited the text and gave invaluable advice for which I am very grateful.

For help given whenever I needed it, I thank Cathy Schling, and Richard Whittell for his clarity and never-failing support.

Sitting in the unfinished coffee bar at 34 Dalston Lane, Tom Holt-Wilson (Centerprise worker) is on the right. Photograph courtesy of Tom Wilson.

1: Making the idea real

A summer night in the late 1960s on Brighton beach. All day Mods and Rockers have been gathering and fighting, and now scores of teenagers are sleeping outside, in danger of being picked up by the police. A group of radical youth workers roam the shore, waking the youngsters up so they can find safer places to bed down.

As the sun comes up, two of these youth workers, Margaret Gosley and Glenn Thompson, are sat in a bus shelter overlooking the sea, getting to know each other and putting the world to rights. Margaret remembers:

> We started to talk about how you could change things if you weren't going to have social work, because we both hated posh people that came in and just made a living off the poor, and changed nothing.
>
> And that's when we started to say, how could you be somewhere like Hackney, in a legitimate way? And we talked about, well what people are there legitimately? And one of the things that came up was, well, shopkeepers are there legitimately, because although they're making a living, they're providing a service. So, you could be there as a shopkeeper.
>
> And then the conversation just evolved, and came around to why were there no bookshops in Hackney? Glenn couldn't understand, when there were all these schools and all these adult education things, why weren't there any bookshops? And I said, 'Well there wouldn't be because, as far as the English class system's concerned, the working classes don't read.' And I remember I said, even as a librarian, I would be nervous going into a bookshop. Bookshops had a sort of aura, they were cathedrals of learning, which was not Glenn's experience at all of course. The sixties revolution, the counterculture, was happening ahead in America, there were bookshops with coffee shops there, but not here.

On the train, back to London, their conversation continued. By the time they arrived back in the capital, Margaret remembers, they had a shared mission, and were falling in love.

Glenn Thompson (24 September 1940 – 7 September 2001) was African-American and born in New York. He didn't learn to read until his teenage years, but when he could he voraciously devoured what books he could lay his hands on. Margaret grew up in Watford, England, and like Glenn, yearned for books as a teenager: "There weren't any books in our house, because you couldn't really afford them then, books were a big expense really. The first boy I ever went out with, we were going to get married, and one of the things we always said is, we're going to have books in our house, and we used to meet in Watford High Street every other Saturday and buy a book."

Glenn worked his passage to Europe on a tanker and did the 1960s version of a grand tour; hitchhiking to Nepal and coming back via Israel where he lived on a kibbutz for two years. Back in New York he worked with a group of young Puerto Ricans on the Lower East Side, helping them learn to read and relate literature to their own experiences, carefully noting how a community project in the area combined enterprise and community work by basing itself within a shopfront café.[6]

While Glenn was on the hippie trail Margaret worked at the British Film Institute as a librarian, and then at the Royal College of Art, which she says was "fantastic" in the 1960s. There was "loads of money" about and the Rolling Stones used to play at the discos. In her spare time, she developed an interest in youth work, volunteering to teach acting at east London youth clubs, although she says "the drama was mostly coming from [the young people] to me rather than the other way round."[7] She first met Glenn when she visited his workplace, the Hoxton Café Project, an experimental youth project based in a coffee bar.

The café had opened in 1963 to give otherwise "unclubbable" kids in Hoxton somewhere to go, hoping to prevent them from becoming even more isolated from wider society. It was open every evening and provided a space for young people to hang out free from adult interference. It was hoped that in time the project would become self-generating, with the customers taking on some of the responsibility for running the café.[8]

By 1968, when Glenn and a fellow American, Nancy Amphoux, were appointed to run the café, a succession of workers had been worn out by the, often conflicting, demands of running both the café and youth project. As experimental youth workers, they wished to avoid exerting power over the young customers, but as café managers they needed to stop them from smashing the place up. What's more, despite the original intention of integrating the isolated young people into the community, the café became known in the area as a "den of thieves" and young people were labelled as delinquents simply for frequenting the place.[9]

Glenn and Nancy became frustrated by the mistrust they sensed from the project's committee, who neither lived in the borough nor worked at the café, and yet controlled the project. Margaret remembers: "Glenn was so fed up with it, and he couldn't understand why these posh English people lived out in the countryside, and ran this café but never came near it. And it was a

---

[6] Toby Taper, 'Report on the First Three Years of Centerprise', c 1974, A Hackney Autobiography, Bishopsgate Institute.

[7] Margaret Gosley, 'Centerprise – Remembering the Beginning' (unpublished, n.d.), Bishopsgate Institute.

[8] Hyla Montgomery Holden, *Hoxton Café Project: Report on Seven Years' Work* (Leicester: Youth Service Information Centre, 1972).

[9] Ibid., 23.

disaster, it was supposed to be experimental, but it never changed."

Something had to be done, Glenn and Nancy decided, and a few months after starting work they handed over control of the project to the young people, only informing the committee after the fact. The committee reluctantly agreed to the experiment for a trial period, on the condition that some of the young people took individual responsibility for the café's management. The trial was not a success, only one young person followed through with their commitment, the electric fires were left on overnight and the police were jumpy about the experiment.[10] In January 1969 the café closed and never reopened.

Giving the young people control of the café project had, objectively, been a failure, but it had succeeded in forcing the contradictions of the project into the open, as former chair Hyla Holden described many years later: "Immediately Glenn challenged the smug, do-good values of the committee … in a way we could not ignore. His restless, enquiring mind immediately got to grips with the real problem, persuading us that unless the project was rooted in the community it had no hope of succeeding."[11] In the months that followed the project's closure Glenn consulted Hyla Holden, along with the young Hoxton Café-ites and John Townsend, youth officer for the Inner London Education Authority (ILEA), about his idea for a new, more "legitimate" project.[12]

More than any other individual, Glenn Thompson dominates the early story of Centerprise. Co-founder Anthony Kendall says "Who do I put it all down to? If you go for one person, it's definitely Glenn. Nothing is ever one person exclusively, but Glenn was the real person who kind of thought about it and worked it out. Lots of people around in the end and all the rest of it, but Glenn was the dreamer who achieved it."

Glenn and Margaret were now married, with a baby daughter Shoshannah, born in 1969. Margaret says Glenn had charm, charisma and "huge integrity" along with a distinctly American "can-do" energy. While Glenn busied himself gathering people around their idea, Margaret says she was "by then supporting Glenn, so he was free to network and talk to people … He was good at it and I was good at earning money, you know. I'm regular, I was a well brought-up girl. Go out to work every day and earn your money."

A core group of young, energetic people quickly formed in the spring and summer of 1969, including Nancy Amphoux, who had worked with Glenn at the Hoxton Café Project, Erika Stern, another community worker and friend of Glenn's from his time in Israel, Anthony Kendall, fresh off a ground-breaking course in social administration at the London School of Economics, and Steve Manning, one of the young people who frequented the Hoxton Café Project. The group went away for a weekend in Newbury, hosted by a wealthy friend of Nancy, to write a manifesto. Margaret remembers "A lot of marijuana was smoked, and a lot of Monopoly was played." They did manage to produce a statement, beginning "we are a group of people composed of who we are". This, Margaret says, reflected the amount of pot smoked.[13] More seriously, it hints at an uneasiness amongst the group

---

[10] Holden, *Hoxton Café Project*.

[11] Hyla Holden, 'Letter from Hyla M. Holden to Centerprise', 6 October 2001, A Hackney Autobiography, Bishopsgate Institute. This letter was written by Hyla Holden to Centerprise on hearing of Glenn Thompson's death in 2001. He concludes the letter: 'I owe Glenn a great deal. Just how much I not at the time realize [sic]. He challenged complacency of every kind and forced me to re-examine my own values; this is never comfortable, but it isn't supposed to be'.

[12] Taper, 'Report on the First Three Years.'

[13] Gosley, 'Centerprise – Remembering the Beginning.'

Glenn Thompson, 1970s. Photograph courtesy of Margaret Gosley.

of founders: who were they to take on this project and what or who did they represent? Despite their disdain for the philanthropy of well-meaning outsiders, most of the group were not themselves from Hackney.

The new project soon had a name: Centerprise, which conveyed the core idea of combining both commercial and community concerns in one building.[14] It was agreed that the project would have a commercial base, but what should the shop be? Apart from a bookshop with café combination, other ideas considered were a travel agency, record shop, launderette or pet shop. The bookshop and café idea won out, perhaps because there was no other bookshop in Hackney since Lucas's of Stoke Newington High Street had closed in the late 1950s. As bookshops were unusual, it would be less surprising to locals that it was more than just a shop, while bookselling appealed most to the group of young radicals setting up the project, who as a group tended to read voraciously, and may have found the work of shop keeping otherwise mundane.[15] Most importantly, the act of creating the bookshop asserted the production and consumption of literature to be a

[14] The name Centerprise, which combined "Centre" and "Enterprise" was thought up by a trustee, Dudley Fishburn, a journalist with the *Economist*, according to Toby Taper's report on the first three years of Centerprise.

[15] Taper, 'Report on the First Three Years.'

"cultural right", that had been denied to working class people by the commercial priorities of publishers, who established shops in more well-to-do areas.[16]

Underpinning the idea of Centerprise was the principle that "the arts, youth and community work, social work and education itself, are not separate entities invariably requiring separate institutions. They are related and inter-dependant."[17] Distinguishing itself from the Hoxton Café Project, Centerprise would not be solely for the deprived but rather it sought to offer a wide variety of things to as broad a spectrum of the population as possible. Intervening in the area without patronising people meant, the group decided, creating opportunities for people to access culture and services otherwise out of reach, denied them by material and cultural deprivation caused by structural inequalities and not due to any fault or deficiency in the people themselves. The café would be a place for exhibitions, music and poetry while the building may be used for meetings, rehearsals, interviews, offices. Centerprise aimed to "encourage the people who have the ideas to carry them out, those who express the needs to learn how to satisfy them."[18] It would be a catalyst for cultural and social action carried out by local people by themselves and for themselves.

By this point, Margaret remembers, "Glenn had said, 'We've got to be real if it's going to happen, otherwise, you know what it's like, you can talk yourself into an idea and then you talk yourself out again. And if it's going to be real, we've got to have an address, and we've got to have a telephone number." The group clubbed together and for £13 a month a small shopfront was rented from Hackney Council on the borders of Dalston, Matthias Road, in October 1970. As a condition of the lease nothing could be sold, but they now had an address to put on the hundreds of letters asking for grants which Margaret typed to trusts listed in the Charities Yearbook. As a new and experimental project, charitable trusts were the most likely to want to fund the new organisation. Centerprise had officially become a charity on 11 May 1970, a legal status that would help it receive charitable funding, and a board of trustees were gathered who could lend the project respectability.[19]

However, in the end it was money from the government that made the difference and allowed Centerprise to start work. When Centerprise applied for funds from the ILEA the idea of combining youth and community work was briefly in vogue, which helped funding be agreed for three salaries and rent.[20] With money starting to come in, a bank account had to be secured. Glenn duly set out to visit Coutts, the Queen's bankers, dressed in jeans and trainers. An account was opened and this typically flamboyant move helped Centerprise later get credit that a smaller bank might have refused to lend.[21]

During the brief six months spent in Matthias Road, the founders built relationships that would sustain the project over the next few years. They "tried to take particular care to find out and establish contact with people, agencies and projects locally and nationally."[22] Anthony Kendall surveyed fifty-seven sixth form students about their attitudes to existing youth services. They

---

[16] Ken Worpole, *Local Publishing & Local Culture: An Account of the Work of the Centerprise Publishing Project, 1972–1977* (London: Centerprise Trust Ltd., 1977), 2.

[17] Centerprise manifesto quoted in Centerprise Trust Ltd, 'Centerprise Annual Report 1978.'

[18] Centerprise manifesto quoted in Taper, 'Report on the First Three Years.'

[19] Ibid.

[20] Hyla Holden (trustee of the Hoxton Café Project) and John Townsend (ILEA youth officer) backed Glenn to the ILEA, giving him the respectability he needed after the disruption of the Hoxton Café Project.

[21] Taper, 'Report on the First Three Years.'

[22] Centerprise, 'Interim Workers' Report October 1970–April 1972', 1972.

encountered the Stoke Newington People's Association, who already organised a newspaper and playgroup in the area and whose members included Ken and Larraine Worpole, who would go on to play important roles at Centerprise. They contacted the Black Unity and Freedom Party, Hackney Citizens Rights Group, statutory agencies like the Probation service, the Chamber of Commerce and similar projects as far afield as Edinburgh. From Matthias Road Centerprise helped two community papers to get going and Nancy Amphoux produced a street pantomime, Puss in Boots, performed by children in local markets.[23]

Despite all this activity, Anthony Kendall remembers those months in Matthias Road as a vital breathing space: "it was just an old shop that had closed down. It had two rooms basically, and a little pub across the road where we spent a lot of time talking about the world and everything else ... But I've always thought it was really great that we had that period. There wasn't a daily grind, you didn't have to get in there, open up the premises, get everybody in and do everything. We had a lot of time just to talk and think. And I think that was really important for the way things moved forward."

In the autumn of 1970, an empty three-storey shop at 34 Dalston Lane, owned by the Greater London Council (GLC), was found to house Centerprise. Margaret describes them "all being excited, because it was an old chemist, and had those little drawers that they used to have, which we all shared out."

The building was in bad repair. Students at the Royal College of Art voluntarily designed its conversion from chemist to bookshop, café, meeting rooms and offices. However, the money needed to pay for the works was held up when one of the charitable trusts that had promised funds delayed their decision. Keen not to lose momentum, the group decided to press ahead with the renovations, doing a fair amount of the work themselves, and spending money on the building work instead of paying out salaries. This decision went against the more cautious instincts of the trustees, who thought that the renovations should be paused while the funds were unavailable but, as would become a running theme, the workers ignored them and pressed ahead. This time it was Erika Stern who managed a series of impossible feats, including persuading the Cadbury Trust, which normally only funded projects in the Midlands, to grant a £1,000 loan for the renovations.[24]

Margaret explains that funders liked the idea that the bookshop would be generating income: "we were doing something, we had proposed visible signs of success, i.e. the bookshop would make some money." However, the charitable trusts wanted a guarantor to underwrite the cost of the book stock in case the shop failed, and until they had one the money was yet again held up. Luckily, Margaret had a friend at the Royal College of Art who knew a millionaire:

> **I'd never met a millionaire before. And he took me and Hilary to Wheeler's, the posh fish restaurant in Soho, and we had champagne cocktails and all the works. I'd never had anything like that before.**

[23] Ibid.; Taper, 'Report on the First Three Years.'

[24] Taper, 'Report on the First Three Years.'

And, he gambled, he took us on to the Palm Beach Casino in Berkeley Street. Hilary and I just drifted around. I remember we went to the ladies there, ever so posh, and we stole a hairbrush each. And when we came out, he had won, and by then it was like, two in the morning, and he gave us each £100 from his winnings. And I remember going home to Glenn, and waking him up and saying, 'I've got £100 Glenn.' And he said, 'Put it on the mantelpiece.' I always remember that. Anyway, he stood as guarantor for the income of the bookshop, which released everything.

Perhaps a more dogmatic group of idealists may have frowned on using connections with millionaire capitalists to finance their dream, but the founders' chutzpah, willingness to take risks and work for free paid off. On 1 May 1971 with a nod to Mayday, the day of the workers, and just two years after the "great manifesto weekend" in Newbury, Centerprise officially opened its doors to the people of Hackney.

Leaflet, unfolded, shows front and back (top) and inside (bottom) promoting Centerprise shortly after it opened in 1971. Courtesy of Tom Wilson.

2: In search of the people

A heady sense of revolutionary possibility permeated the atmosphere of the early 1970s. Liesbeth de Block, who would later teach adult literacy at Centerprise, remembers: "young people's opinions and voices and aims and passions were listened to. Thinking about it now, the difference for young people is enormous. Then we felt that we could change things. We fucked up but we did have this feeling of possibility and change, although it was in the background of a lot of battle." This feeling was partly inspired by revolutionary movements abroad. Margaret Gosley wrote "there was Che Guevara and Castro of course, and everyone in the streets of London seemed to be wearing a black beret with a silver star."[25] The fight against apartheid in South Africa, revolutionary movements in Latin and Central America and anti-colonial struggles in Africa, were "part of your life in a way", Liesbeth says.

A trickle of young idealists was arriving in deprived inner-city areas like Hackney, seeking to put into practice radical new ideas about education and social work. They worked as teachers, social workers and youth workers, often living in some of Hackney's many "hard-to-let" council flats, communes or squats. Margaret wrote "our ideas of popular revolution centred around Illich and the idea of network rather than hierarchy; and Freire and his politics of literacy."[26] In his 1971 text *Deschooling Society* Ivan Illich critiqued institutionalised education and proposed alternatively that it should be self-directed and organised through informal, peer-to-peer networks. Paolo Freire was a Brazilian educator and philosopher whose writing on critical pedagogy, most famously in *The Pedagogy of the Oppressed*, was just becoming known by English-speaking readers in the early 1970s. Richard Gray, a newly trained teacher who arrived to teach in Hackney in 1972, describes himself as a "disciple of Freire". He says "his whole approach to education was like music to my ears, because it depends on what the learners bring to the classroom, or the teaching situation. And he just said it so eloquently, that it's not about doing things for people, it's not about leading the people, it's about taking what the people are interested in, what their concerns are, what matters to them, and for the intellectual who wants to work with them, to be at their service. It's a dialogue. It's up to you to actually work alongside people."

[25] Gosley, 'Centerprise – Remembering the Beginning.'
[26] Ibid.

Schools, strikes and newspapers

Hackney was fertile ground for those in search of people to work alongside. By 1970 it was a distinctly working class area with an ethnically diverse population, housed in the borough's large stock of social housing. The borough was counted amongst the most deprived areas of Britain. Incomes were low, unemployment high and housing inadequate, with 20 per cent of residents without a bath and 16 per cent without hot water.[27] Younger people were moving out of Hackney, leaving a diminishing, aging population behind. Meanwhile new immigrant populations were making Hackney their home, with people from the Caribbean, Cyprus and the Indian subcontinent joining the longer established Jewish and Irish communities.

Industry in Hackney had traditionally been light; furniture-making, the rag trade and shoemaking were all prevalent. There were some large factories too; a workforce of 1,500 at Lesney's factory in Hackney Wick made Matchbox toys until 1982.[28] By the time Centerprise was opening in the early 1970s these traditional industries were beginning to decline. A decade later a writer documenting "life under the cutting edge" of Thatcherite Britain would describe Hackney, somewhat pessimistically, "as the home of dying industries and increasingly marginalised workers".[29]

Barry Burke and Ken Worpole wrote in a Centerprise publication in 1980: "political movements and forms of organisation do not arrive completely by surprise, nor spring from the earth unseeded. Although different periods are marked by a different intensity of political change, some seeming much more dynamic than others, there is always some thread of continuity."[30] Hackney had a vibrant history of trade unionism, propagandism and protest. In the Reverend C. M. Davies's 1873 book *Heterodox London* Hackney was dubbed "the most heretical … of the various quarters of the metropolis".[31] Hackney workers had taken part in the reform movement for adult suffrage, and had helped to set up the International Working Men's Association. The borough's workers, organised in trade unions, had joined the General Strike in 1926 and housed the hunger marchers of 1932 in local churches and the public baths.[32] Young women on strike from the Rego and Polliakof clothing factories had roamed the streets singing for their strike pay in 1928. Open air debates in Victoria Park in the early part of the twentieth century were still talked about by older people, while the anti-fascist battles before and after World War II were well remembered, especially by the Jewish community. Nationally and locally organised industrial action was still very much a feature of life in 1970s Hackney, hospital workers and teachers struck in 1973, Turkish clothing workers in 1974 and Borough nursery nurses in 1975.[33]

Working class social life often revolved around workplaces, pubs, working men's clubs and neighbourhoods where extended networks of friends and relations lived close to each other. Increasingly these proximities were disrupted by industrial decline, the post-war demolition of terraced housing and development of council estates. As Annie Spike, a housewife and night

---

[27] Centerprise Trust Ltd, 'Centerprise Annual Report 1978.'

[28] Margaret Willes, *Hackney: An Uncommon History in Five Parts.* (Hackney Society, 2012).

[29] Paul Harrison, *Inside the Inner City: Life under the Cutting Edge*, Repr., with new foreword and corrections, Penguin Politics & Current Affairs (London: Penguin Books, 1992), 51.

[30] Barry Burke and Ken Wolpole, *Hackney Propaganda: Working Class Club Life and Politics in Hackney 1870–1900* (Centerprise Trust Ltd., 1980), 7.

[31] Cited in ibid., 10.

[32] Barry Burke, *Rebels with a Cause: The History of Hackney Trades Council 1900–1975* (London: Hackney Trades Council: Hackney Workers' Educational Association, 1975).

[33] Ibid.

cleaner who contributed to the Centerprise book *Working Lives: Volume Two 1945-77* (1977) put it: "They say the working class are selfish, but if they want to know the truth they should come and live with us ... they build them [new flats] so that we can't live with one another and be friendly. But we try to be friendly on the streets."[34]

While the area was certainly not devoid of cultural facilities, there was nothing quite like Centerprise in Hackney when it opened. Jacqueline Rose wrote in the *Hackney Gazette* to welcome the new initiative: "No one can fail to notice that Hackney has not got many recreational amenities. For example, there are hardly any coffee bars open late at night, and there is a crying need for bookshops. Folk who study at evening class and work during the day may find that they have to go up to Holborn in the West End to get a book."[35] For some young people, growing up in Hackney in the early 1970s with a taste for the counterculture, the traditional youth clubs and church Sunday Schools meant to entertain them did not appeal. Neil Martinson, a school student at the time Centerprise opened, describes how he experienced the Hackney of his adolescence as a "cultural desert". The half dozen cinemas he remembers from his childhood were mostly closed down by the time he was a teenager and "there wasn't a lot to do. There was a period of time when I went to a Jewish youth club in the East End, down in Aldgate, the Oxford and St George's, which my dad went to, but I never really fitted into that, it didn't quite work for me." "Unclubbable", intellectual young people like Neil would be some of Centerprise's first loyal customers, eagerly making use of the books, facilities and free space to hang out.

Students from Hackney Downs grammar school, including Neil Martinson, were involved in the production of an alternative magazine, irreverently titled *Hackney Miscarriage*. Alternative publications were massively popular; there were *Oz*, *Private Eye*, *Ink*, *International Times*, *Time Out* and an extraordinary number of locally produced community newspapers. Another one of this young group, Neil Littman, explains that they made *Hackney Miscarriage* as part of a wider rebellion: "We had a bit of a rebellious streak in those days. We were all sort of what I call proto-hippies. And we all thought we were being alternative. We all wanted to make our mark. And our way of doing it, by today's standards, was fairly innocent – through the written word. And in way it shows that we thought we could change things."

Centerprise gave the young people some money to publish *Hackney Miscarriage* and helped them with layout. Neil Littman remembers typing his contribution, a music review, on a typewriter upstairs in Centerprise's offices. The students got involved in every stage of the production process, as Neil Littman describes: "I remember Letraset type. I seem to remember it involved some kind of carbon paper impression on it and paper being churned through a roller. I remember the pasting up of the artwork was done with little bits of paper with glue. I remember the smell of it."

Neil Martinson described the first edition, in an interview recorded in 1984: "The cover was brilliant, it was Ted Heath who was Prime Minister then

[34] *Working Lives: A People's Autobiography of Hackney. Vol. 2: 1945–77* (London: Centerprise Trust Ltd., 1977), 114.

[35] Jacqueline Rose, 'Mainly for Women', *Hackney Gazette*, 8 June 1971.

in a tank, looking out at a soldier and there's a bubble, and the bubble said 'if you piss down here once more I'll blow your fucking head off'. It was all that kind of stuff. And there were things in it like secret school reports, children's rights; I reviewed *The Little Red Schoolbook*. There were two issues, a thousand copies each, that sold out."[36]

Hackney Miscarriage could not have been produced within the school, Neil Littman explains: "I think there was a feeling that our school would have imposed censorship on what we were doing. We were trying to be anti-establishment, in our own little way. And to do that, we did it outside, and yet the irony is I believe that some of our English teachers were involved in it as well. So, they were probably, I dare say, at risk of losing their jobs if they had been found out. So, the whole thing had the feeling of a sort of clandestine, secret operation about it. And I think that's what made it attractive." When the first magazine came out, Neil Littman describes how a "storm erupted at the school. Absolute mayhem. It was banned". The head teacher at Hackney Downs, Neil Martinson said "accused Centerprise of being a Maoist cell, which it wasn't by any stretch of the imagination."[37]

There was a smattering of strikes by students in schools across the country at the time, inspired by the student unrest of the late 1960s and counter-cultural publications like *The Little Red Schoolbook*. Margaret Gosley was by then working as a librarian in Hackney Downs School, having taken the job to be closer to Centerprise. She remembers the students going on strike: "they decided to have a protest and they all went and sat on Hackney Downs, on the playing fields, with their arms folded, singing 'We shall overcome'. But they timed it all wrong, because they started at the beginning of the dinner hour so by the end of the dinner hour they were all worn out, tired, and they'd missed their dinner. And it was really easy to get them back in to school again."

In the adjoining borough of Tower Hamlets, at Sir John Cass's Foundation and Redcoat school, the "Stepney School Strike" broke out on 28 May 1971. The cause of the dispute was poetry, as unlikely as that might seem. English teacher Chris Searle had been suspended for publishing an anthology of students' poems, *Stepney Words* (1971), that the school's conservative management had deemed too 'drab' and 'gloomy' a view of East End life.[38] Searle's suspension provoked a strike of eight hundred students who demanded he be allowed to return and made headline news. Eventually he got his job back, but Chris Searle maintained: "In coming out for me the children were really coming out for themselves. It was their poetry and their lives that was the issue, and not my disobedience."[39]

At Hackney Downs, the rebellious students found affinity with a few sympathetic staff members like Ken Worpole and Margaret Gosley. Neil Martinson reflects on the importance of these relationships: "By the time I was about fourteen or fifteen, the teachers were introducing us to a whole load of ideas. Probably they'd be struck off now I suspect, or put in prison. So, for example, one of our teachers was Ken Worpole, he was my English teacher, and he introduced us to the ideas of people like William Morris. We went to

In search of the people

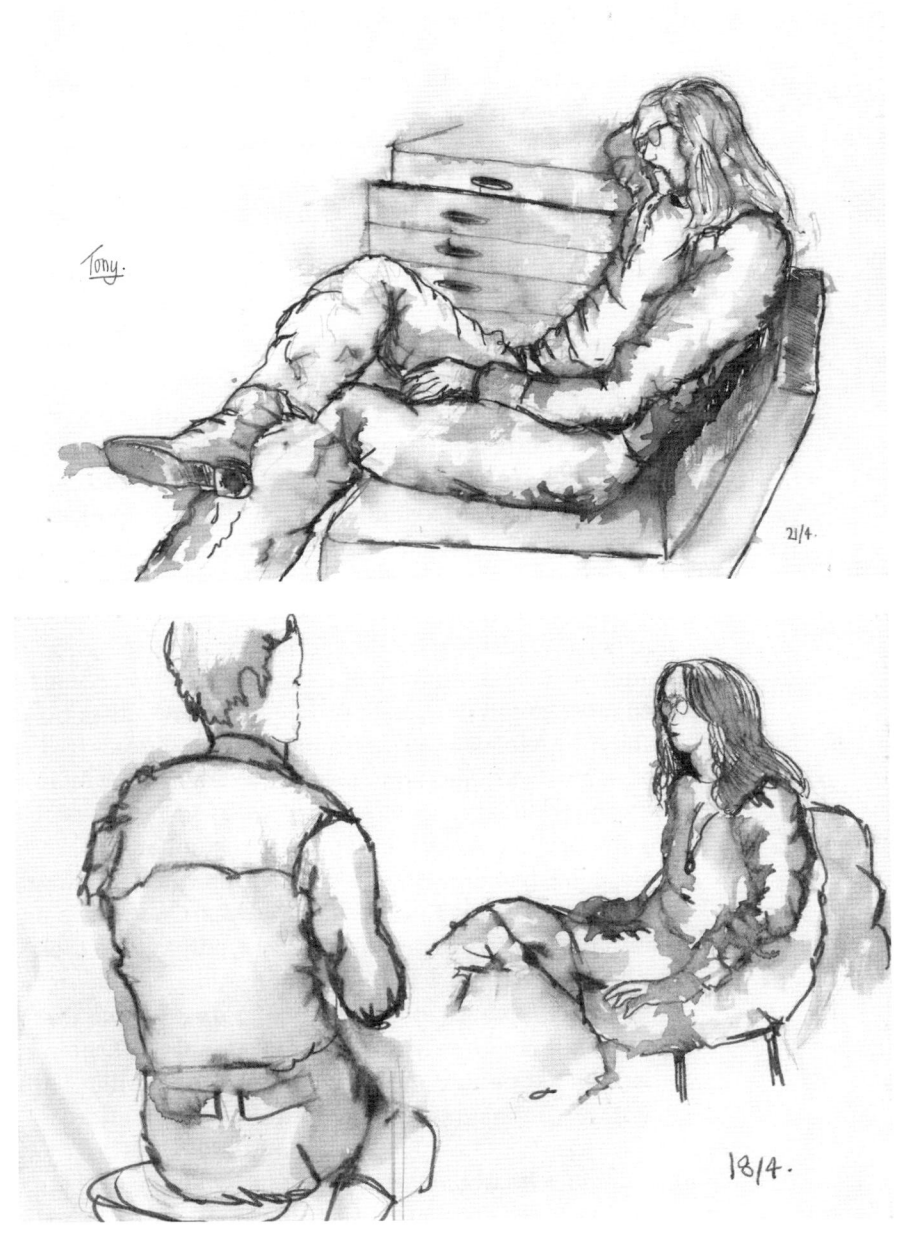

Sketches by **Neil Littman**, Centerprise customer. **He** remembers: "I was studying art A level. I used to do drawings, daytime and evening. Every time I went to Centerprise there was something to do if I wasn't reading a book." Copyright © Neil Littman.

see jazz. I mean the idea of a teacher taking you to see jazz now, would be frowned upon I suspect. You had a post-1968 generation of teachers teaching then who were very radical. And by the time I was about fifteen I had kind of lost interest in school and I was quite anti-establishment, so I had rejected things like exams and stuff like that. So, we used to spend a lot of time in the library talking to Margaret, about ideas and books and reading."

Ken Worpole, who taught English at Hackney Downs School from 1969 and later became Centerprise's first publishing worker, describes the late 1960s as a time of innovation in education, particularly in the teaching of English:

> It was a very idealistic time, and it was very important in developing the ideas that enabled me to think about what I might do when Centerprise happened. There were two things that were very strong in the 1960s in teacher education. One was the idea that the child is full of innate creativity, and a lot of that's suppressed by traditional forms of teaching, which is pumping external knowledge into them, and denying their own sense of identity and self.
>
> And that's related to the second thing, which was particularly of importance to English teachers, which was that the reading books we were using in the classrooms to teach people to read, the language, the vocabulary and the imagery was completely at odds with most young people in Britain. We were rather po-faced about it at the time, we were all very judgemental. I don't feel so bad about it now, but, we raged against Ladybird books for their suburban, very stilted lifestyle, father with a trilby hat and a pipe and so on. We shouldn't have got so hot under the collar.
>
> So, these two things were very strong in our understanding of what the role of the English teacher was. One was to allow the young person to express themselves, and to take their life and their experiences as valid; and the second thing was to bring about change in the nature of educational publishing so that it reflected much more accurately what was happening in Britain, certainly what was happening in Hackney when I arrived in 1969, which was that it was becoming a multicultural part of London.

Oliver Flavin, who would become a youth worker at Centerprise in 1975, first taught English at Edith Cavell school in Hackney. He arrived from Ireland at the age of twenty-one, already a qualified teacher, and so was not all that much older than his students at first. He remembers scouring black bookshops like New Beacon Books for reading material to use in his classes and even attempted writing poems in Caribbean English himself. He says:

> I quickly realised content was more important than, the length of the words for instance. Like, if you hit on something that the kids saw as being about them, that they could identify with, they would tackle something theoretically way beyond their means, way

beyond their ability. Whereas if you churn something out, like "the cat sat on the mat", then they may be able to tackle it slightly better but it wouldn't turn them on.

I can remember vividly I came across this poem called "To the black mother" in a book from New Beacon Books, that was written out in a dialect. So, during lunchtime, I had the classroom to myself and I wrote it up on the blackboard. And then as my first class came in, they started to find their desks and one of the girls stopped and looked, and started to read. And, it was like an electric shock had gone through her, and, I think her friends must have immediately wondered what was going on, and she was sort of, half saying it aloud. So, then she went back to the beginning and they all started to read it. So, after about three minutes, most of the class were sitting down really reading the poem that was on the blackboard.

And by coincidence, a deputy head teacher came in to the classroom, and, he must have wondered what was going on, because everybody was just looking at the blackboard. Eventually, when he realised that they liked this poem, he asked this girl called Hyacinth to read it out, and she read it aloud, really proudly. She realised it was sort of, for her, both as a girl and as a young black woman. So, she read it out, and, everybody looked at the deputy head teacher, and he said, "Oh that's very nice. What does it mean in English?" There was a mass sucking of teeth.

Not all students welcomed attempts by white teachers to change the syllabus on their behalf. Richard Gray remembers one of his students dismissing his attempt to teach him black history, gleaned from books supplied by Centerprise, saying "We no want dis ras-clat ting from no white-man teacher. Give we Nelson and Wellington, like everyone else."[40]

Teachers like Richard and Oliver came to Centerprise in search of the books they needed to make their teaching relevant to their working class, ethnically diverse students. Others began to create their own books and, like Chris Searle in Stepney, to publish writing by their students. Centerprise, Glenn in particular, would eagerly support this development, seeing it, as Ken Worpole wrote, a "natural development for a community project based on a bookshop".[41] In 1973 a project dedicated to publishing was established at Centerprise, with its origins in the publications first brought to Centerprise by teachers and students from Hackney Downs school. That it was children's writing that kicked off the publishing project is no coincidence, children had always been central to the Centerprise project of widening access to books, not least through the bookshop. In 1975 the Centerprise collective wrote that "in educational and cultural circles all kinds of moral and character defects are attributed to people who don't have books in their houses, or who fail to buy them for their children, yet the practicalities of book-buying outside of the West End are always forgotten."[42]

---

[40] Richard Gray, 'What Centerprise Means to Me', tumblr, *A Hackney Autobiography*, accessed 21 October 2016, http://a-hackney-autobiography.tumblr.com/post/120543214489/what-centerprise-means-to-me-by-richard-gray.

[41] Ken Worpole, 'About Hackney: Community Publishing at Centerprise', *East London History Group Bulletin*, n.d., London Borough of Hackney Archives.

[42] Centerprise Trust Ltd 'Report on the First Year's Work in the New Premises at 136 Kingsland High Street London, E8. June 1974 – May 1975', 1975, London Borough of Hackney Archives.

Centerprise chess club. Copyright © Ken Worpole.

On Dalston Lane

A little off the beaten track but well served by buses, 34 Dalston Lane was where Centerprise first opened its doors in 1971. Awaiting partial demolition and road widening, the street became increasingly desolate in the early 1970s, creating space for community organisations to set up home, including Freeform Arts, Hackney Task Force and Hackney Pensioners' Association. Close by, the Four Aces, a much-celebrated night club played cutting-edge black music in an old circus building, now demolished.[43]

Inside Centerprise, 34 Dalston Lane had "a lovely muggy atmosphere" says Robin Simpson, who worked there from 1974. Toby Taper, who wrote a report on Centerprise in 1974 described how the old chemists with "its dark wooden shelves and mirrors provided just the right setting – a somewhat chaotic private library compiled almost entirely of brightly coloured paperbacks; there was a feeling that you will find exactly what you want, but which no one else knew about."[44] Children's books were given almost a third of the space until February 1973, when a separate children's bookshop was opened down the road at 66a Dalston Lane. School student Neil Littman visited regularly. He says: "I thought it was fantastic. When you walked into the front it was just books, and then on the left hand side at the back, there was a kind of seating area and on the right hand side there were counters for selling stuff, but there was also a hatch where you could order food. Later, when I got involved in *Hackney Miscarriage* I found out there were offices upstairs as well. So, I got to use the facilities and I did eventually get to know the whole building because of going there so frequently. I think at one point I was going there two or three times a week."

Glenn ran the bookshop, negotiated favourable rates from publishers and suppliers and set up bookstalls at schools and playgroups to entice parents and children into the shop.[45] Richard Gray, a local teacher, came in to look for teaching materials and felt instantly welcomed and charmed by Glenn, if a little overawed:

> I walked in and browsed round the books. And there was this very cool guy over by the till who was Glenn, it was pretty evident that he was the leading light of the place. I remember his Afro, and I remember his Cuban heels, and his cool jeans, and his leather jacket, and I thought he was so cool. He was like I imagined Malcolm X or Stokely Carmichael or Bobby Seale, you know, Black Panthers. And he was American. I was a bit in awe of him, I have to admit.
>
> I looked around, and, I found this *Cultural Action for Freedom*, by Freire, and took it to the till, and Glenn was delighted that somebody was buying this. … And he said, "Hey man, it's great to rap with you," all this kind of thing. And I just thought wow, I like the place. It was a really friendly atmosphere.

Toby Taper's report on Centerprise described the coffee bar as less

---

[43] Dalston Lane has been written about by Patrick Wright in *A Journey Through Ruins: The Last Days of London* (2009, updated edition). See also Aaron Williamson's *Splitting the Atom on Dalston Lane: The Birth of the Do-It-Yourself Punk Movement in March 1977* (2009), which tells the story of a Dalston punk band in the context of its times.

[44] Taper, 'Report on the First Three Years.'

[45] Ibid.

successful than the bookshop at first. It was seen by some as exclusionary, she wrote, "like a club 'lurking' behind a curtain at the end of the bookshop" used predominately by Hackney's "idle youth": amongst them the "intellectual unclubbables" who produced *Hackney Miscarriage*.[46] It was small, with just one large table for customers to gather around but hosted an impressive fifty exhibitions in its first three years. *Time Out* encouraged the use of the exhibition space, saying "the spectators are challenging. … It could give new outlets to artists, together with friendly advice and specialist knowledge about the local scene."[47] The notice boards were full of information, and the space was used for live music and poetry readings. A record player that you could play your own music on, and board games like chess, gave the place a homely, casual atmosphere.

On the opening day, a street parade organised by community worker Erika Stern roamed the area to let people know Centerprise had arrived. As it was a little tucked away, it was necessary to draw people into the building. Simultaneously it aspired to reach out across Hackney, acting as a "catalyst" to help kick start new projects. This broad remit led to the new centre involving itself in a vast number of initiatives in the three years it spent on Dalston Lane.

Centerprise's founders had kept their mission statement deliberately vague as they hoped to be responsive to the community in which it was situated. What Centerprise did would be determined by "the kind and quality of interest aroused and the kind and quality of need which becomes apparent." There was to be a "continuous search for local groups – new, old and undreamed of – to combine with, or to connect to each other to sell ideas to."[48]

Anthony Kendall, who had been appointed as one of Centerprise's three full-time workers in October 1970, describes how they attempted to get local people involved through a plethora of new projects that often "started from Centerprise and moved outwards". These included community activities on local estates, playgroups and summer schemes for young people and independent initiatives supported by Centerprise like Hackney Playbus and the Lenthall Road photographic and silk screening workshop.

Local groups and projects were offered access to meeting rooms and office facilities including a typewriter, phone, duplicator, photocopier, and a van. Groups were encouraged to use Centerprise for no more than two meetings in a row as it was hoped that the building would act as an incubator to help new projects off the ground. There were some exceptions made, especially for groups that met in the daytime when there was less demand for rooms, such as the Squatters' and Claimants' Unions.

Some new projects took up residence inside the building, like the advice centre that Anthony helped start with Hackney Citizens' Rights Group. They set up a rights stall in Ridley Road Market on Saturdays that directed people in need of help to a weekly advice session staffed by volunteers at Centerprise. A 'Learning Exchange' was started by Dorothy Wise to facilitate local people swapping skills, inspired by Ivan Illich's radical ideas about

[46] Ibid.

[47] 'Listing', *Time Out*, 1 October 1971.

[48] Taper, 'Report on the First Three Years.'

Jud Stone teaching Community Studies at Centerprise in the early 1970s. Photograph courtesy of Jud Stone.

education outside of institutional settings. Centerprise also supported local, radical newspapers, for example *Hackney Action*, which later became *Hackney People's Press*, and made use of the building and facilities.

Centerprise hosted educational courses, often through the newly formed Hackney Workers' Educational Association (WEA), which drew new groups of people into the building.[49] The Hackney WEA branch had been re-established around the same time as Centerprise opened, organised by many of the same people. Centerprise hoped to run courses through the WEA, financed by the larger organisation. However, this idea was undermined by their insistence on providing their own tutors, whether they were in possession of formal qualifications or not. This policy was the cause of a lengthy battle with the central WEA and meanwhile Centerprise often ended up subsidising the courses. These were often less traditional and generally did rather better than the officially sanctioned classes. Neil Martinson remembers: "So they had some stuff on the history of jazz, which my mate Steve Horigan did, and memorably got George Melly along one evening to talk about it, completely drunk, but very, very, very entertaining. So, I mean there was a kind of combination of things. Some of it was definitely political, some of it was cultural."

A Community Studies course hosted by Centerprise for City and East London College taught a group of teenage Post Office workers. Students were sent out to do various forms of community work, both within Centerprise and further afield. They cared for elderly people, worked in playgroups and helped produce publications, gathering at Centerprise in the afternoon for discussions. These teenage students found themselves in an unusual learning environment. The tutor, Jud Stone, remembers how they aimed "partly to integrate the kids into Centerprise. They would come in and I would introduce them to all the workers in the project that were there and I do remember Sheila Greenwood was working in the café then. She was an amazing woman and one of the girls – they were pretty young, about fifteen, sixteen, was pregnant. And Sheila used to make her come in and sit down in the coffee bar and give her a glass of milk every Thursday, before she did anything else. I think she decided that she didn't have breakfast and she should. Things like that that you don't expect as part of your education."

The early 1970s were a time of a new kind of political struggle, based in local communities and seeking to radically change the structure of everyday life, as Centerprise wrote in 1978: "Spilling over on a truly international scale was the growth of a 'counterculture', the black movement and the women's movement. The focus of political struggle changed dramatically, and new forms of political action emerged. Squatting groups, community groups, claimants' unions, community newspapers, 'alternative' magazines, black groups, nursery groups, women's groups proliferated."[50]

As Centerprise was just one organisation active at a time of much, often interconnected activity it can be hard at times to disentangle what precisely its impact was. For example, Centerprise wanted to increase the number

---

[49] The Workers' Educational Association (WEA) had its roots in the adult education movement at the turn of the century. Founded in 1903 with the aim of providing adult education to ordinary working people who were ill-served by the existing school system, it ran classes in partnership with trade unions and offices. The WEA provided the tutors, and courses would not be approved unless they allowed class discussion as part of the learning process. Although this was a more equal and participatory approach than earlier forms of adult education, the basic format of middle class tutors designing and delivering the curriculum remained in place.

[50] Centerprise Trust Ltd, 'Centerprise Annual Report 1978.'

of preschool playgroups in the borough. Maggie Driscoll, who worked full time at Centerprise from January to December 1972, produced an exhibition for the coffee bar on playgroups which was displayed in April 1972, and showed what existing provision there was, what the benefits were and how parents could set one up. Centerprise also stocked materials for playgroups to borrow. Later, 136 Kingsland High Street would provide office space for the umbrella groups Hackney Under Fives and Hackney Play Association. However, while Centerprise undoubtedly played a part in the movement to improve facilities and childcare for under-fives, it was not the primary source of energy put into this area, and without Centerprise, Hackney Under Fives and Hackney Play Association would have existed regardless.[51] Anthony Kendall reflected that: "If you were a real politician you'd claim that the whole lot was because of you. In reality, quite a bit was, but it was you and others. But the fact that Centerprise was there, as a kind of ideas catalyst, absolutely helped."

Centerprise involved itself in numerous projects in these first few years with mixed results: there were some great successes while other projects dropped quietly by the wayside. No decision was formally made about whether it was to be a liaison service for community activity across the borough or if it wanted to work on a neighbourhood level itself.[52] Centerprise workers and students on placement worked intensively to kick start projects in various localities. It was expected that Centerprise would develop partly in response to the workers "noticing some sort of need" and "partly from the ideas of the users"[53] but where Centerprise workers went into local areas to start projects it was considered to be especially important that in time the people living in the places concerned came to lead the project themselves.

In her report on Centerprise, Toby Taper noted sardonically that while its workers like Anthony were a "natural source of leadership" this could be "unfortunate in a situation where the objective was to help the community to rely more on itself." Anthony Kendall, she wrote, "In some ways strode into Hackney much as his ancestors had gone off into distant parts of the empire to bring the British way of life to the natives."[54] More than forty years later, Anthony Kendall still remembers being described in this "less than flattering" way. Like many of the people involved in starting Centerprise, Anthony was not from Hackney. He spent much of his childhood in Egypt, where his father worked for Shell. At a young age, he witnessed the 1952 revolution and the "British being chucked out" in the Suez Crisis of 1956. Back in England he attended various private schools, and left with few qualifications until he went to the London School of Economics to gain a Diploma in Social Administration, where he took part in the student unrest of 1968. While his class and background may have set him apart from many people in Hackney, Anthony reflects that the years he spent at Centerprise involved him deeply in community life, leading him eventually to become a local councillor, and in the early 1980s leader of the Council, but also creating a profound personal connection to the place. He says "Hackney was the first place I had lived in

[51] Taper, 'Report on the First Three Years.'
[52] Ibid.
[53] Centerprise, 'Interim Workers' Report October 1970 – April 1972.'
[54] Taper, 'Report on the First Three Years.'

for any longer than five years, because of my father's job. And Hackney was the first place where I actually put some roots down."

One project lauded as a great success was the Haggerston Community project. Haggerston estate, a short distance south of Dalston, was an especially rundown and depressed place. According to an article in the newspaper *Hackney Action*, "people on the estate feel they have been dumped there and that the only concern of the authorities is the collection of the rent – whether or not services thereby paid for are rendered."[55] In September 1971 concerned probation and youth officers called together a meeting of groups, including Centerprise, to discuss the estate's problems. The idea developed of running a community project which would "pay one full-time worker to do some of the initial donkey work in helping tenants to set up various projects that would be run by themselves."[56]

Centerprise had the capacity to respond very quickly and offered the services of a student on placement, Jane Sturner, to help the project along, opened a bank account for the project and helped fundraise. Jane discovered a need for play facilities on the estate, amongst other things, and in response, Maggie Driscoll started a mums and babies group while local parents were trained up as playgroup leaders. Centerprise secured a £1,000 grant and the Haggerston Tots playgroup was open daily and parent run within a year.[57]

A paid community worker, Peter Chambers, commenced work in October 1972. He started a food co-operative, partly to engage with residents. The co-op offered basic goods at cost for estate residents, serving at least a hundred regular customers. A short film made by the BBC shows sugar and cornflakes being unloaded by children from Centerprise's van and brought into a ground floor flat on the estate. "Power to the People" is written on the wall above the shelves and a *Hackney Gazette* notice proclaims "Rent Strike on Haggerston". A queue of women forms, eager to buy their weekly shop for around half the cost of prices found elsewhere.[58]

The community project did not immediately morph into a resident-led initiative, as was intended. In March 1973, Peter Chambers wrote self-critically on the front page of *Hackney Action*: "For the first few months of the project the worker was very concerned about the role he was playing i.e. that of a social worker, every one of which, as we know, carries a government health warning. Nothing was really thrown back at the tenants to deal with."[59] Conscious of this, he encouraged tenants to petition for repairs themselves and was encouraged when this started to happen. The tenants' demand for repairs culminated in a rent strike, which won the most active group of tenants rehousing elsewhere. This was a great success but undermined efforts to build a community organisation on the estate as many active people then moved out.

In July 1973 *Hackney People's Press* reported that the food co-op had closed, after local shopkeepers protested at the cut-price competition and their landlord, the GLC, ordered them to cease trading from their property.

---

[55] Peter Chambers, *Hackney Action*, 5 March 1973.

[56] Ibid.

[57] Taper, 'Report on the First Three Years.'

[58] *Hackney Food Co-Op*, 1973 (BBC, 1973), https://www.youtube.com/watch?v=spExIZBd72Q.

[59] Chambers.

At the same time, the tenant who had taken over running the food co-op singlehandedly had been rehoused after the rent strike, which made its future uncertain. Despite the usefulness and popularity of the project, no other tenant stepped forward to run it. This meant that Peter Chambers wasn't too concerned about the closure: it "didn't matter much, both because it did not matter to the tenants and it was not a tenant initiated project."[60] It is possible that the women who found the food co-op to be a low-cost way of feeding their families may not have had the time or felt they had the skills to run it themselves. It is also unclear whether a local coordinator would have been paid, as Peter Chambers was, for their time, or if they were expected to work voluntarily.

By June 1973 Peter Chambers was elated, a group of ten tenants were willing to take over the management of the community project. A Haggerston Tenants Council was formed and in 1974 Peter Chambers left the project in their hands. The Haggerston Community Project was judged a great success because it was taken over and run by local people, although many similar initiatives failed to achieve the same result.[61]

Glenn is remembered by many as Centerprise's central figure in its early years, although a large team of workers and volunteers, too numerous to fully mention here, all contributed to what it became. The first group of workers were committed in principle to working collectively, but their working culture prioritised getting things done over more time-consuming processes of collective decision-making. The possibility that strong personalities amongst the founders could come to dominate if they "hung on too long" was something that Glenn and the rest of the group were well aware of, as Ken Worpole relates: "our joke was always that the first thing you do when you go to a new organisation, is shoot the founder. Because if they hang around they're always looking over your shoulder."

If Centerprise was to be the catalyst for community development in Hackney, the founders were meant to be the catalyst for Centerprise, which once established would either be taken over by the community or left to collapse of its own accord. Margaret remembers the initial group resolving: "Number one, we wouldn't make a living out of servicing the needs of the deprived; and number two, we wouldn't just let it go on for us, it wouldn't become a thing that kept us alive. So, we said right from the beginning that, we, if we did do anything like that, it was only going to be for three years."

These three years were intense. The full-time workers, including Glenn and Anthony, worked on average seventy-hour weeks, according to Toby Taper. A larger team of "part-time" workers were expected to work a thirty-five-hour week, although in practice some worked less while others put in almost as much effort as the full-timers.[62] Anthony explains that at times he disagreed with Glenn about the workload: "Glenn would give 150 per cent, he would be there every Saturday, he'd be there Sunday if we were open on Sundays, and I used to try and limit my Saturdays, and was very happy to do one Saturday a month in the bookshop or whatever. And when there were

[60] Peter Chambers, 'Haggerston Food Co-Op Closed down', *Hackney People's Press*, July 1973.

[61] Taper, 'Report on the First Three Years.'

[62] Ibid.

community activities that took place on a Saturday I'd do it, the advice stall on Ridley Road Market was always a Saturday. But I was not prepared to give up the whole of my weekend all the time, which Glenn was much more likely to do."

Margaret Gosley and her daughter Shoshannah Thompson. Photograph courtesy of Margaret Gosley.

Like anyone else working those kind of hours, Glenn could only dedicate himself to Centerprise, and its seventy-hour week because he was supported in other areas of his life, in particular by Margaret who was looking after their daughter Shoshannah and supporting him emotionally. Margaret writes how, after her two months of maternity leave from the Royal College of Arts ended, she would take Shoshannah to work with her. "Every morning I wrapped [Shoshannah] in her coloured blanket and we got on the 73 bus to South Kensington. It was a long bus ride and if possible I would sit at the front where you could feel the heat of the engine and the two of us would go to sleep."[63] Margaret says "six months later I had hepatitis very badly and was in hospital for a while, and I think that's why, because I was wiped out, I was knackered really."

Centerprise was slowly transforming into a co-operative. In February 1973, the original trustees had handed over formal control of the organisation to a larger co-op group made up of local residents. By 1974 Centerprise

[63] Gosley, 'Centerprise – Remembering the Beginning.'

was preparing to move to bigger premises, while Glenn and Anthony were planning their exit. A Centerprise meeting held on 8 October 1973, accepted news of Glenn's resignation with "the greatest reluctance" and resolved that "in these circumstances, they would need to take a more committed part in the running of the project."[64]

Margaret remembers the time of transition as being one of "terrible sadness". Around the same time that Glenn left Centerprise, their marriage also ended. Margaret made a "total break" with Hackney, at least for a while, leaving her job at Hackney Downs School to work for the ILEA. Glenn went on to work at Penguin before co-founding the Writers and Readers Publishing Co-operative, most famously publishing the *For Beginners* series that provided accessible introductions to a wide array of topics. Centerprise moved into a double-fronted shop on the much busier Kingsland High Street, just around the corner from Dalston Lane. It would be here that the original vision of a place that fused commercial and community concerns would have the space to really take form.

[64] Centerprise Trust Ltd, 'Minutes of Centerprise Trust Ltd Co-Op Group, Monday 8 October', 8 October 1973, Arts Council of Great Britain Archive.

Centerprise workers including Chris O'Mahony (left), Maureen Johnson (centre) and Jackie Murdock (right) on Kingsland High Street outside Centerprise, 1980s. Photograph courtesy of Maggie Hewitt.

3: Buildings have history

On the frontline

At Centerprise's Annual General Meeting in November 1974, secretary Sheila Greenwood reported: "it seemed hard to believe that Centerprise could exist outside the Dalston Lane premises; and certainly there are some things that have been lost forever in the move, notably the informality and what some of the kids call the 'cosiness' of the first shop."[65] Centerprise's new home at 136–138 Kingsland High Street, was in the heart of Dalston's bustling shopping area. The increase in passing trade meant customers started to come in "spontaneously", Robin Simpson says. Centerprise's 1978 report described how "in the High Street the shops had to adapt quickly to the noisy, undifferentiated multi-racial shopping crowds who were likely initially to be less interested in the long-term aims of Centerprise than in its ability to provide an efficient and friendly service in the two shops."[66]

Gary Molloy, who lived around the corner from Centerprise as a child in the 1970s, explains that Centerprise really stood out on the high street:

> When we moved into the Shellgrove estate in 1976 all the families were from similar backgrounds. The women would have been working as dinner ladies, the guys would have been electricians, my dad was a carpenter. The local pubs were really, really busy and, there was a really big community of similar type people. There wasn't really anyone that would be classed as intellectual or middle class, upper middle class; there wouldn't be people that would stand out as a bit different and a bit creative or arty.
>
> ... You'd just go past Centerprise and there might be someone there with a polo neck on, a beard and just talking quite posh. And everywhere else there was caffs, and down Ridley Road was just packed full of the fruit sellers, and the women would be talking to each other and everyone had a trolley. And then you'd get to Centerprise, and it would be a little bit different.

In some ways, with its wood floors and toys for children to play with Centerprise, Gary says "was like a middle class kind of place, which you see now,

[65] Sheila Greenwood, 'Secretary's Report to the Centerprise Trust Ltd AGM', 11 November 1974, Arts Council of Great Britain Archive.

[66] Centerprise Trust Ltd, 'Centerprise Annual Report 1978.'

but way back then. So, it was way ahead of its time. And people would talk, would be having discussions, quite meaningful chats and, you know, it was like a real intellectual type place."

Dalston was a place people gathered to shop, socialise and talk politics. Ridley Road Market, close by, functioned on Saturdays especially as a sort of "Speakers' Corner", Ken Worpole says, with rival left wing groups selling newspapers and religious groups spreading their messages.[67] When the evening came, Dalston was a centre of black nightlife, from blues parties held in people's houses, the outdoor gathering spot of Sandringham road, to the famous Four Aces night club. Local resident Pauline Brown remembers: "When you're passing through Sandringham Road, you feel like you've been to a party already. … Because the vibes were so energetic … Sandringham Road was just a hop and running place. These guys, they want to bring in the real Jamaica."

Sue Shrapnel[68] said it was a "running theme" in 1975, when she joined Centerprise, to question why more black people didn't use the building, despite Hackney's growing African-Caribbean community. After the 1977 firebombing of Centerprise by the National Front, Sue said "I think [Centerprise's standing in the black community] turned around. I think it was just like we were also in the same frontline they were in." It helped, she thought, that staff from Centerprise were seen taking part in anti-racist demonstrations: "I don't think it was a kind of heroic deal. But I think it was important, I think it was one of those moments in the world where you're either for us or you're against us, and I think we succeeded in falling on the right side of that line."[69]

Ken Worpole remembers that in the later part of the decade "there was a very nasty atmosphere in the streets of Hackney and east London, really nasty, and violent." By 1978 Centerprise reported they had experienced an increase in political violence in the area directly: "we have had our windows broken four times, racialist slogans sprayed on the building, an arson attempt and provocative incursion by known members of the National Front."[70] Jud Stone recalls that for a while staff and supporters slept in Centerprise in case it was attacked again.

The National Front's headquarters were located on Great Eastern Street in south Hackney, from 1978 until the early 1980s.[71] The far right did not go unopposed, a strong anti-fascist movement organised counter-demonstrations, marches against racism and summer concerts. On one of these demonstrations held in Southall, west London on 23 April 1979, Blair Peach, an east London teacher and friend to many at Centerprise, died. Witnesses saw Blair in a side street being hit on the head by police officers from the Special Patrol Group.[72] Just the day before the demonstration Blair had bought books in the shop and Centerprise was shut down for the day of his funeral.

Threats from the far right continued sporadically into the 1990s. Claudia Manchanda, who worked in the coffee bar relates that in 1990: "We got picked on by an organisation that was post-National Front called Combat 18,

---

[67] Ken Worpole, Oral history interview with Ken Worpole, 8 March 2010, Hackney Museum, http://museum.hackney.gov.uk/object9637.

[68] Sue Shrapnel later changed her name to Sue Gardener.

[69] Sue Shrapnel, Interview with Sue Shrapnel (later Gardener) by Maggie Hewitt, 5 December 1984, A Hackney Autobiography, Bishopsgate Institute.

[70] Centerprise Trust Ltd, 'Centerprise Annual Report 1978.'

[71] https://hackneyhistory.wordpress.com/2012/05/11/the-national-fronts-hackney-hq/

[72] 'Blair Peach Inquiry Ruled Out', 13 April 1999, http://news.bbc.co.uk/1/hi/uk/317775.stm.

Damage to the Centerprise bookshop after an arson attack in August 1977. This fire was contained by prompt action taken by passers-by. Image courtesy of London Borough of Hackney Archives.

The Lime Green Mystery

Above and right: **Michael Ferreira's funeral procession on Stoke Newington High Street, 1979. Michael Ferreira was nineteen years old when he died in custody in Stoke Newington Police Station on 10 December 1978. Photographs copyright © Alan Denney.**

Buildings have history

and somehow they had got our personal details, and everyone that was mixed race received a really horrible letter in the post, hand delivered with blood on it, saying, 'Racial mixing make you want to hate, rape or murder.' And it had pictures of people hanging on hanging trees. And I had that put through my door nearly every day for about a week. And, we went to Stoke Newington police station, and the police laughed. And we had to walk each other home."

Apart from the extreme and highly visible violence perpetrated by the far right, racism was experienced in multiple forms by black people living around Centerprise, permeating many if not most of their interactions with the state. A Commission for Racial Equality report in 1984, *Race and Council Housing*, said that institutional racism meant black people were allocated the worst housing by Hackney Council.[73] Most perilous, especially for young black people, were dealings with the police; from their constant use of the "sus" laws to stop and search them to the high number of deaths associated with the borough's police force. These included Aseta Simms, a mother who died from head injuries while held in custody in Stoke Newington Police Station on 13 May 1971; Michael Ferreira, nineteen years old, who died on 10 December 1978 after running into Stoke Newington police station for help after being stabbed in a racist attack, twenty-one-year-old Colin Roach, who died of a gunshot wound received in the foyer of Stoke Newington police station on 12 January 1983 and Vandana Patel, who was killed by her husband in the police station's Domestic Violence Unit in 1991.[74]

Janet Rees, who worked at Centerprise's advice centre from 1979 to 1985 describes how "young black men who knew the police was looking for them would sometimes come into Centerprise and ask me to take their photograph. And so, I would take their photographs, and then ring the police station saying, 'I've got so-and-so here, he's coming in, because he knows you're looking for him. I've just taken his photograph. There's not a mark on his body.' You know, he hasn't got any bruising, his limbs are all intact. Because, they feared that going into the police station would be a beating-up for them."

These tragic deaths were marked by struggles for justice waged by the victims' friends and families, supported by community organisations such as the Black Unity and Freedom Party and Hackney Community Defence Association, a self-help group established in 1988 and Centerprise. Photographs by Alan Denney show a crowd of hundreds of mourners marching through Stoke Newington and Dalston as part of Michael Ferreira's funeral procession. After Colin Roach's death, the Roach Family Support Committee called for an inquiry, a demand supported by frequent protests.[75] An independent inquiry, commissioned by the Roach family themselves, was eventually held and an influential report, *Policing in Hackney 1945–1984*, was published in 1989.

In 1981 riots took place in inner-city areas across the UK and Dalston was no exception. Centerprise opened to provide people with emergency legal

---

[73] Commission for Racial Equality, 'Race and Council Housing in Hackney. Report of a Formal Investigation Conducted by the Commission for Racial Equality into the Allocation of Housing in the London Borough of Hackney', January 1984.

[74] Black Unity and Freedom Party, 'Who Killed Aseta Simms?', 1972, https://hackney-history.wordpress.com/2016/09/11/who-killed-aseta-simms-1972/; Harmit Athwal, 'Black Deaths in Custody', 11 November 2002, http://www.irr.org.uk/news/black-deaths-in-custody/.

[75] Roach Family Support Committee (London, *Policing in Hackney, 1945–1984: A Report Commissioned by the Roach Family Support Committee* (Karia Press/RFSC, 1989).

CUT UP DUB

Wind blows cold,
Feet shuffle in the dark,
Apprehensive of Babylon
Touring the streets for the brethern.

A goin' bounce up Stokey tonight,
But a h'aint goin' run through the night.
You see Babylon got a thing:
(Nigger running in the dark) = CRIME
"Hey boy, what have you just done?"
"Me hafficer? - Nat a ting."
"Why you running then?"
"Late sa', gotta meet de dartah."
"Sorry son, going to have to take you in,
Lots of crimes in this area,
Come on down to the station for questioning."
Nex' morning, black boy come from station,
No bookings, no charges,
Jus'a heapful a bruises.
Man, a' goin' bounce up Stokey tonight,
But a' h'ain't goin' run in de dark.

Detail of "Cut Up Dub" by Hugh Boatswain from *Talking Blues*, published by Centerprise in 1976. Copyright © Hugh Boatswain.

advice and first aid.[76] Gary Molloy, who was a child at the time, remembers Centerprise being one of the only buildings on the High Road which was not boarded up. Its large windows remained unscathed while the shoe shop across the road was looted by local children. Unrest continued on a smaller scale throughout the early eighties, with clashes with police especially fierce on the 'frontline' of nearby Sandringham Road.

After the move a new attitude was needed amongst the Centerprise collective as the "sheer size of the place" on the high street, secretary Sheila Greenwood worried, made it possible that people could "sail along making a hash of things" without anyone noticing.[77] The workers devised and implemented new practices of collective working, with longer meetings and more emphasis on collective scrutiny. Centerprise was now more visible and there was an increased pressure to be seen as professional. As Sheila said, "now that we are in the High Street we need to be able to supply what our customers require of us": answering the phone (so that people would stop calling her at home, she hoped), keeping the place "usable and clean", observing fire regulations, paying bills and opening the shops on time. Shelia urged "I think it is time we all, staff and members, stopped clinging to our amateurish habits and really started functioning efficiently instead of dreaming dreams – well, as well as rather than instead perhaps, but with the dreams kept firmly under control."[78]

Not only was the new building significantly more expensive, but also, as the project became more firmly established, the money received from charitable trusts, who preferred to fund experimental work, began to run out. A report on the first year in the new premises prepared by Centerprise wrote that all the other major funders, including the charitable foundations, the ILEA and the GLC "thought that the major responsibility for supporting Centerprise belonged to the local authority."[79] In 1975 the Greater London Arts Association (GLAA) and the Arts Council met Centerprise to discuss the funding deficit, and offered to help by pressuring Hackney Council to step up its support.[80]

However, at first Hackney Council was not at all inclined to support Centerprise. When it opened in 1971 the borough librarian had produced a somewhat hostile report concluding: "The activities undertaken to date parallel similar activities organised by the Council at a much more professional and effective level … it is difficult for me to recommend any substantial aid to the organisation to enable it to undertake similar activities." He suggested that Centerprise "may be fulfilling some wider social need" and could therefore approach a different committee for funding for this.[81] As this suggests, Centerprise's combination of arts and community work sat awkwardly with the way that the Council viewed the purpose of arts funding in the early 1970s. Funding for organisations which provided social services was kept separate from arts and leisure as the latter were not perceived as having any social purpose.

Centerprise fared better later in the decade as new funding priorities

---

[76] Centerprise Trust Ltd, 'Centerprise Annual Report', 1982, A Hackney Autobiography, Bishopsgate Institute.

[77] Greenwood, 'Secretary's Report to the Centerprise Trust Ltd AGM.'

[78] Ibid.

[79] Centerprise Trust Ltd, 'Report on the First Year's Work in the New Premises at 136 Kingsland High Street, London, E8. June 1974 – May 1975'.

[80] 'Notes on a Meeting between the Arts Council (Neil Duncan, Charles Osborne and John Buston), the GLAA (Michael Bakewell, Literature Panel and Lawrence Bayliss) and Centerprise.', 12 February 1975, Arts Council of Great Britain Archive.

[81] London Borough of Hackney, '4th October 1971 Minutes Libraries and Amenities Committee Vol. 4', February 1971, HAD/LBH/L/8, London Borough of Hackney Archives.

were gradually adopted by Hackney Council. Influenced by the progressive funding agenda of the GLC, the new approach favoured community arts, projects reflecting London's multi-ethnic communities and expected arts and cultural activities to have a social purpose. Hackney Council gradually began to offer leisure services that might appeal to ethnic minority communities. In 1976 the libraries began to stock books in Gujarati[82] and in 1977 an exhibition was made of Caribbean literature, borrowed from Centerprise.[83] Although it did not represent a specific ethnic minority, Centerprise's broad and inclusive remit allowed it to benefit from this shift towards multiculturalism.

By 1978 Centerprise had a "much happier relationship and funding policy" with Hackney Council, which with the ILEA were now the main funders of the project.[84] Centerprise was also funded by the Greater London Arts Association (GLAA) and received sporadic support from the Arts Council, who were at times ambivalent towards Centerprise. An invitation to Centerprise's fifth anniversary celebration in 1976 kept in the Arts Council's archive has had "I went to this, god help me" written across it by an unknown hand.[85] An internal Arts Council memo sent in 1978 describes Centerprise as presenting "the usual community arts muddle of arts and social service." Nevertheless, the same memo worries that the "dedicated people" they found there worked in "ill-equipped, not very clean and not very warm offices" and suggested increasing their grant.[86]

The bookshop, coffee bar and publishing project generally all turned healthy profits, or at least covered their costs, and so Centerprise had more financial independence from grant makers than most community organisations. However, the Centerprise Annual Report of 1982 wrote that the aspiration of its early years for "financial independence" which they had hoped would "ensure political autonomy" was now seen as impossible to achieve. They realised that "Centerprise could no longer function without massive subsidy in grant aid" and continued, "our greatest insecurity comes from the threats currently posed by Central Government to abolish the local State as we know it."[87] By 1986 Hackney Council was Centerprise's largest single funder, the GLC a close second, followed by the Greater London Arts Association and the ILEA. However, also in 1986, the GLC was abolished, soon followed by the ILEA, and the ability of local authorities to fund community organisations was increasingly restricted by central government. Funding from Hackney Council became increasingly important as other funding sources dried up; in 1996 making up 52 per cent of Centerprise's income, including trading turnover.[88]

[82] London Borough of Hackney, '4th February 1976 Minutes, Libraries and Amenities Committee Vol. 6', 76 1975, HAD/LBH/L/12, London Borough of Hackney Archives.

[83] London Borough of Hackney, '2nd March 1977 Minutes, Libraries and Amenities Committee Vol. 9', 77 1976, HAD/LBH/L/14, London Borough of Hackney Archives.

[84] Centerprise Trust Ltd, 'Centerprise Annual Report 1978'.

[85] Harriet Tod, 'Letter from Centerprise to Charles Osbourne at the Arts Council', 20 April 1976, Arts Council.

[86] 'Arts Council Internal Memo from Secretary General to Literature Director on Centerprise', 6 March 1978, Arts Council of Great Britain Archive.

[87] Centerprise Trust Ltd, 'Centerprise Annual Report 1982'.

[88] Centerprise Trust Ltd, 'Centerprise Annual Report 1996', 1996, A Hackney Autobiography, Bishopsgate Institute.

The Lime Green Mystery

136 – 138 Kingsland High Street
Hackney E.8   tel. 254·9632-5

Centerprise

coffee bar

Community Centre
Free Meeting Rooms
Advice Centre
Local Publishing
Local Reading Centre
Playgroup &
Youth Centre

bookshop

Left and above: **front and back of leaflet advertising Centerprise, 1970s. Copyright © Doffy Weir.**

Behind the shopfronts

Approaching Centerprise from the street the first thing to be spotted was the distinctive lime green colour of the building. A list of some of the projects found inside were painted between the two doors, leading to the coffee bar and bookshop: Community Centre, Free Meeting Rooms, Advice Centre, Local Publishing, Local Reading Centre, Playgroup & Youth Centre. Oliver Flavin remembers: "it was quite a smart building, particularly compared to the old Centerprise, smart, green frontage, lovely wooden floors."

In just the first few months the building housed jumble sales, concerts, older people's meetings and children's activities.[89] In 1975 an adult literacy initiative, Hackney Reading Centre, took up residence on the top floor, next to the publishing project's office. One floor down, the advice centre and many local groups made use of the meeting rooms, while a public office provided continued to offer facilities to anyone who needed them. There was space to host a few other organisations; Hackney Under Fives and Hackney Play Association had offices, Hackney Workers Educational Association held some of its courses at Centerprise, and in 1978 the Hackney Girls Project was set up with Centerprise as its base. In the daytime, the 136 Playgroup used the basement, at night youth groups took over, a folk club met regularly and the large space hosted meetings or concerts. Robin Simpson remembers the building as buzzing with activity: "I remember feeling so proud, that you opened a room, and in one it would be a bunch of kids playing the piano, in the coffee bar would be all these kids playing chess, and in another room, it would be a Chile Solidarity Campaign meeting, in another room there'd be lawyers giving advice."

The shopfronts offered customers anonymity, as Robin Simpson relates. Advice centre customers could pop in as if they were just coming for a coffee, and reading centre students could visit the building without risking the world at large knowing they could not read and write. Co-operative member and customer Larraine Worpole says: "that was the brilliant thing about it, which was Glenn's vision, he had obviously seen this working in New York, you have a building where you go through the door, and there are all these different places, and there's no stigma. I mean for example, when you go to claim benefit, everyone queueing up along the road, you're going in there like you're broke and you're victimised already before you even get through the door."

All the projects within Centerprise benefitted from the possibilities for interaction the combination of projects housed within the building opened up. For example, publishing worker Maggie Hewitt describes how being based in Centerprise and taking turns working in the bookshop and coffee bar, meant publishing was "demystified in a way. Otherwise we'd have been stuck up on the top floor and we could have been anywhere." The publishing project wrote in Centerprise's 1982 Annual Report that working in the shops meant they kept closely in touch with the readers, as well as the writers of

89
Greenwood,
'Secretary's Report to
the Centerprise Trust
Ltd AGM.'

their books. The books they published were sold directly from the bookshop, the coffee bar hosted book launches and readings. Would-be authors in general, they said, found Centerprise an approachable place to visit and enquire about publishing.[90]

Visitors from near and far came to tour the building and learn how the project worked. In 1983 there were eighty-four such guests, including organisations from the very local, "Dalston Community Centre Project", to the international: "New York Literacy workers" and forty individual guests, many from abroad.[91] Centerprise was the subject of many articles, theses and documentaries, including a rather serious film made for German television, which Robin Simpson remembers included "profile shots [of the workers] as we strode down Kingsland High Street, gazing into the middle distance". Each part of Centerprise reached out to similar organisations further afield through umbrella organisations like the Federation of Radical Booksellers, the Federation of Worker Writers and Community Publishers, the national literacy magazine *Write First Time*, and local affiliations of community organisations set up to share expertise and fight funding cuts. In this way Centerprise sought to spread its work beyond Kingsland High Street and Hackney, and feel part of a wider political project.

[90] Centerprise Trust Ltd, 'Centerprise Annual Report 1982'.

[91] Centerprise Trust Ltd, 'Centerprise Annual Report 1983', 1983, London Borough of Hackney Archives.

WOMENS NON FICTION   WOMENS

The bookshop

If you were the first to open up in the morning, Judith Skinner, who managed the bookshop from 1993 to 1999, remembers "you lifted the great heavy shutters at the front of the building. On the café side, the first person who got there, up with the shutters. Up with the shutters, which were really heavy. The door to the bookshop had a shutter on it. Get those up. Horrible job, heave."

Through the bookshop window was a display of books, that often crinkled up at the edges when the damp seeped in behind the glass. Behind the window was a large selection of children's books. Through the internal door with the coffee bar the smell of food cooking and customers' cigarette smoke seeped through. Centerprise's own publications were displayed prominently. At the back of the shop on the left were some of the political books, kept tucked away because it was felt people who wanted them could go and find them. Also in stock were paperback novels, radical literature held on sale or return, Open University text books, cookery books and anything else that might appeal to the diverse local readers the shop served. Card racks hung on a shelf, displaying postcards, some made by the Centerprise Young Photographers' Group, and a selection of badges sold well. Rosie Ilett, bookshop worker from 1984 to 1988, says "I mean I'm sure if I saw it now I'd think it was really small, but it seemed quite big. There were thousands of books."

In 1974 to 1975, its first year on the high street, the bookshop had a turnover of around £32,000, representing sales of around 75,000 books.[92] The bookshop was extremely well used by local people, especially by local school teachers, parents and nurseries for its extensive selection of children's books. Centerprise brought bookstalls into schools, and sent them specially prepared newsletters, promoting books deemed suitable for "multi-ethnic Britain".[93]

Rosie Ilett says the customer base in the 1980s was "really mixed", encompassing Hackney's growing middle class, people involved in "miners' strike support groups, peace movement things, feminist politics," and people using other parts of the building. Janet Rees, who would later work in the advice centre, remembers her first visit as a customer: "Oh it just felt like coming home … It was like your best friend had sorted out some books for you to read."

[92] Centerprise Trust Ltd, 'Report on the First Year's Work in the New Premises at 136 Kingsland High Street, London, E8. June 1974–May 1975.'

[93] Centerprise Trust Ltd, 'Centerprise Schools' Newsletter', 2 July 1978, London Borough of Hackney Archives.

Left: bookshop customers browsing, early 1990s. Copyright © Sherlee Mitchell.

Roger Mills, a local school leaver who joined writing groups at Centerprise and published his own work there, remembers his first visit when he was "struck by the way that the local books were given prominence. I think they were near the door. So, rather than looking at the more mainstream commercial fiction they had there, it was the local books that were presented as the face of Centerprise, which I think was interesting. And also, offbeat publications like magazines and things that you didn't see anywhere else, political or cultural books that you wouldn't see anywhere else. So, it didn't look like Foyles. It looked more alternativey."

Some customers used it as "a kind of a community resource in the way that we would see a library", Rosie says. This was true for Neil Littman, who describes how the bookshop widened his access to literature:

I grew up in a house with very few books. I think that was a reflection of my parents' lack of education. It wasn't intentional. It wasn't like they were saying you can't have books. I mean, when I asked for them, they bought them for me. I was also an avid reader at the library in Hackney. But I actually managed to read everything in the children's section, moved onto the adult's section and read copious amounts of material there, but, I'd run out of things to read.

And when I went to Centerprise, they had a much more contemporary selection. Much fresher. I remember the books I did read there, and they were nearly all in the poetry section and were all by people like Adrian Henri, Roger McGough, the Liverpool poets, and they resonated with me because they seemed to be talking directly to me and about experiences that I understood.

And one thing Centerprise allowed me to do, which probably was not helping their sales really, was I used to pick the books up and read them, and put them back. So, I was effectively using Centerprise as a kind of reference library.

Dealing with shoplifters is remembered as the least pleasant part of working in the bookshop. Workers were often fraught with worry about whether, how and when to approach people stealing books. People might steal books for all sorts of reasons, as Janet Rees remembers: "This one character used to come in a lot. One day he called me over, and he had been stealing all these feminist books, and he had underlined the things that he thought were really offensive to men, and he handed them to me, these books. And he had been sitting in the coffee bar, working his way through all these feminist books that he had stolen from us, and he very much wanted me to know that he found these things offensive."

How the bookshop was stocked was the result of specific decisions made by bookshop workers, who had to balance commercial and political priorities and somehow be both a community and general bookshop. Oliver Flavin, who worked at Centerprise from 1975 relates:

I remember people would get cross because their favourite book

wasn't being promoted in the bookshop. But you then have to decide, are you going to have lots of these [kind of books] on display, or are you going to have your latest Penguin bestseller? You know, the publishers will be looking for you to take these big display cabinets of *The Bermuda Triangle* or whatever the latest bestseller would be.

And if you were too much like a local bookshop, then you didn't serve the need of the community to have a good general bookshop. And if you were too much like a general bookshop, you didn't serve the need of the community to promote its own embryonic writing and publishing and so on. So, we compromised.

In 1978 the collective argued that being a general bookshop that stocked a wide range of books meant they were left "open to criticism" for selling books by authors who were considered sexist or racist.[94] However, as their overall aim was to be as accessible to as many people as possible they felt they needed to stock a range of popular reading matter, which was not always as politically correct as they might like. By 1986 this had changed, the bookshop was committed to routing out any books with racist or sexist content, guided by a bookshop users group.[95] Rosie Ilett says that in the 1980s:

> there was a view that, because it was very much a community bookshop, and it was an anti-racist, non-sexist inclusive bookshop, that it was really important that there was nothing in there that people could take offence at. Now, that's really difficult, obviously, because people could take offence at anything. And, you know, where do you draw the line? But there were certain things we wouldn't stock. I mean this is so obvious, but we wouldn't stock something like *Mein Kampf*, obviously, like, why would you? I can remember having debates about this, like, would we order it if it was a customer order? Now that person could be doing a PhD on the influence of those ideas on, say, the National Front, so arguably it's completely appropriate that person reads that book. But there was a lot of sensitivity around that whole idea of, are there books that if we stocked them, it would be condoning them, or it would be somehow dangerous and offend people, or it will somehow bring ideas to people that perhaps we shouldn't be doing, we shouldn't be the purveyors of these ideas.

The bookshop aimed to provide books of interest to the diverse communities living around Centerprise. In the 1970s the bookshop worked with specialist adviser Rosemary Stones, who helped them develop their children's section to include better representation of ethnic minority writers and characters. In the 1980s bookshop workers, Rosie says, debated whether to sell "children's books that were seen to be really white or not have enough black characters in them. There would be debates around why weren't we

[94] Centerprise Trust Ltd, 'Centerprise Annual Report 1978.'

[95] Centerprise Trust Ltd, 'Centerprise Annual Report 1986', 1986, A Hackney Autobiography, Bishopsgate Institute.

At night Centerprise might fill with people for book signings, talks and readings from a range of authors, from the local to the famous, sometimes both, organised by the bookshop and publishing project. Amongst the many writers hosted over the years were Raymond Williams, Ngugi Wa Thiong'o, Nawal El Saadawi, Linton Kwesi Johnson, Andrea Levy, Gillian Slovo, Rosa Guy and Merle Collins.

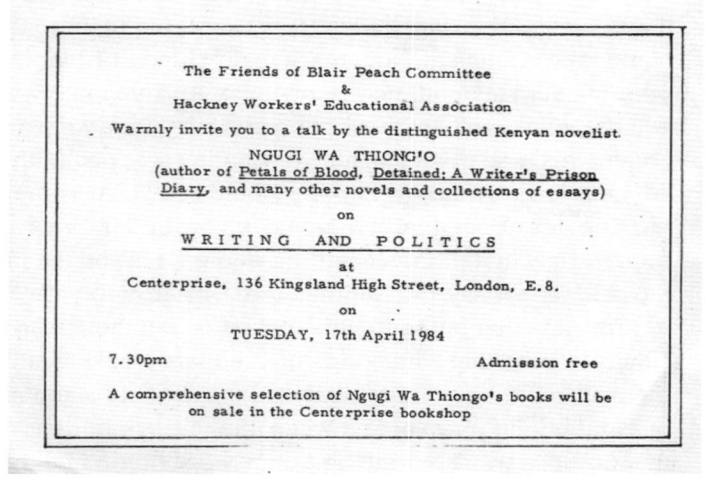

WORKERS' EDUCATIONAL ASSOCIATION

Hackney WEA & Centerprise
GUEST LECTURE
In order to raise funds for the Centerprise appeal

RAYMOND WILLIAMS
Professor of Drama, Jesus College, Cambridge

'POPULAR FORMS OF WRITING'

Friday, January 8th, 1982   7.30p.m.
At Centerprise   £1.50p

Centerprise Trust Ltd.

The Friends of Blair Peach Committee
&
Hackney Workers' Educational Association
Warmly invite you to a talk by the distinguished Kenyan novelist
NGUGI WA THIONG'O
(author of Petals of Blood, Detained: A Writer's Prison Diary, and many other novels and collections of essays)
on
WRITING AND POLITICS
at
Centerprise, 136 Kingsland High Street, London, E.8.
on
TUESDAY, 17th April 1984
7.30pm   Admission free

A comprehensive selection of Ngugi Wa Thiongo's books will be on sale in the Centerprise bookshop

Invitations to two talks at Centerprise with academic Raymond Williams and author Ngugi Wa Thiong'o, 1980s. Courtesy of Ken Worpole.

Centerprise bookshop's re-opening after refurbishment with special guest author Rosa Guy, c. 1983. Photographs courtesy of Maggie Hewitt.

A FEAST OF LEAVENED BREAD
****

In this bookshop of ours

The books, though wrapped in a rainbow's prism,

Don't stand in their parti-coloured rows

To be picked

And sniffed at

Like pretty flowers

But like earnest tin-loaves, half-risen

From sifted flour

Wait to be shifted and eased

Into a good oven's heat

Till, gently tapped and fork-pricked,

They give out that low, answering hum

Are proven and done

With all this yeast bubbling at hand,

We, having fed and grown stronger,

Understand our power

To kneed between finger and thumb

Will know how to make dough

Into a feast, a plentiful spread

Of leavened new bread

PS Not to mention the pink-iced cake
   That will take longer

Lotte

for Maggie a little conceit

getting any more authors in that were more inclusive or books that had more black characters, or more black authors? But, you know, the reality was at that time, it was still very early days for British black writers to be published." Something debated at Centerprise, as elsewhere, was whether there should be separate sections for books by black and women writers. Judith Skinner says the bookshop had an extensive black fiction section when she worked there in the 1990s. She reflects on this choice that: "it's arguable, do you have a section that's labelled black, or do you say black writers are writers, and everyone needs to see those books and let's have them everywhere? We chose to have a section that was black fiction. Because there were people who were looking for black fiction, and that was where they looked. And, I still don't know really what the right answer to that is. Because otherwise, how do people find those books?"

Rosie describes how the workers aimed to stock diverse reading material in all sections of the shop: "So for example, it would be really important that the cookery section had loads of stuff that would be resonant for, say, older black women in the community, that it wasn't all Mary Berry or something equivalent. There was a couple of importers of books from Jamaica that we would use, where we would get books that people really did know from home, and weren't available in Waterstones."

In 1988 Rosie was ready to move on from Centerprise. She reflects that by then there were more options for book buyers, even in Hackney, than when Centerprise opened its doors in 1971. Up the road Stoke Newington Bookshop was now open, providing a general bookshop for the area. Further afield chain bookshops like Waterstones were taking off, stocking books by feminist and left wing publishers like Virago, Women's Press and Pluto Press. Despite this increased competition, the bookshop continued to make a steady profit over the years. By the early 1990s, bookshop manager Judith Skinner reflected that, while Centerprise may have struggled to attract the lunch-hour trade she had hoped for, they had a "very loyal clientele".

Left: a typed poem given by Lotte Moos, member of the Hackney Writers Workshop, to Maggie Hewitt, publishing worker at Centerprise. Courtesy of Maggie Hewitt.

Centerprise coffee bar, 1980s. Photograph courtesy of Maggie Hewitt.

The coffee bar

The smell of food wafted into the bookshop through the open archway that led to the coffee bar. In the 1970s the aroma was coffee and quiche, replaced in the 1990s by Caribbean delicacies: jerk chicken, baked snapper fish and delicious roti. Covering one wall was a large noticeboard, full of useful community information. The rest of the wall space was taken by ever changing exhibitions, often mounted by local artists. People wandered in through the bookshop or straight from the street, got a coffee, stroked one of the cats that the children loved to play with and rested for a while, away from the bustle of Dalston.

Claudia Manchanda co-ran the coffee bar with Erita Crawford in the early 1990s. She describes the sights and sounds of a typical day:

> In the morning it was very peaceful and people would come in for tea. There was always a lot of humour. And we'd always be cooking. It was an open-plan place, the counters and cookers were waist high, everyone would see what we were cooking. At lunchtime, it was heaving with local people coming to get their rice and peas and jerk chicken, and dumplings, or snapper fish. And, in the afternoon, again it would be more quiet with regulars that would come in and have a cup of tea and talk, play dominoes. We'd have the radio on. People would even dance sometimes.
>
> A very big mishmash of people. Sometimes school kids would come in after school to have a snack. Or they could just come and sit in and not have anything. It was that kind of atmosphere, that anyone could just come in. If it was cold, people would just come in; if it was raining, people would come in. People would look at the books in the bookshop and come and sit in the café. The atmosphere in the coffee bar was, just nice, jovial and safe.

In the very early days there were such basic cooking facilities in the coffee bar that worker Sheila Greenwood remembers doing a lot of the cooking at home. For instance, she took the left over rolls and milk home in the evening, and baked them into bread pudding to serve the next day.[96] In the 1970s and early 1980s the main fare was filled rolls, soup, a daily hot vegetarian meal and cakes baked by people at home and sold on to the café. All Centerprise workers took turns to work in the coffee bar, meaning the quality of its food

[96] Sheila Greenwood, Conversation with Rosa Schling, August 2016.

varied, as reading centre tutor from 1982 to 1986, Chris O'Mahony, remembers: "It was hard not to always cook the same thing, because you knew you could. And, we also used to ask who's in the café today, because we knew who were the better cooks." Advice centre worker Janet Rees admits: I'd been cooking this bean salad for about two years before someone told me it was dreadful. I had very wholesome tastes you see, so I just assumed everyone else did, but they clearly didn't."

Some workers specialised in managing the coffee bar, like Roy Akong, who is remembered as being a good cook and making "little ray of sunshine soup". In 1986 two-part-time workers took over its management, Erita Crawford and Patrick Cafferty.[97] Erita Crawford would continue to run the coffee bar for many years. In 1989 she was joined by nineteen-year-old Claudia Manchanda, and both worked full time.[98] By this point the coffee bar sounds highly organised, as Claudia describes: "The coffee bar was open Tuesday till Saturday. Me and Erita would meet at eight in the morning, and buy thirty snapper fish and maybe fifty pieces of chicken. We'd make a pot of rice and peas, we'd make jerk chicken, we'd make baked snapper fish. We'd make a tray of carrot cake, a tray of banana cake, a big thing of coleslaw. And we'd serve teas and coffees all day, and juices. And, basically it was a public space that we ran, it was actually more of a homely space, but we did make a profit, and local people loved the food. The quality of the food was second to none, it was amazing Caribbean food."

[97] Centerprise Trust Ltd, 'Centerprise Annual Report 1987', 1987, A Hackney Autobiography, Bishopsgate Institute.

[98] Centerprise Trust Ltd, 'Centerprise Annual Report 1990', 1990, A Hackney Autobiography, Bishopsgate Institute.

Erita Crawford with a volunteer called Elvis, early 1990s. Copyright © Sherlee Mitchell.

The food was so good some people would travel specially to buy it, like Judy Joseph who visited Centerprise regularly for their expertly made roti that "brought back Trinidad". She remembers the café staff as "Caribbean women who were just beautifully clean and well-presented behind the counter. And then there were all these various Caribbean foods, including, this particular dish which is called a roti. And, I remember thinking, mm, rotis are normally horrible, my experiences of having them [in Britain] are horrible, but I will have a go, I'll actually taste these. So I bought a roti, brought it home, and it was absolutely delicious."

While the food changed over time the atmosphere remained welcoming and informal. The coffee bar was a hub for local people, who could read the newspapers provided, use the noticeboard and view the exhibitions of art and photography on display. It was used by every other part of the building – as somewhere to meet and talk, to take tea breaks in and use as an impromptu waiting room. In the evenings, the space would fill up with people for book launches, readings or regular events like the Word Up Women's Café, held in the 1990s.

In 1978 the coffee bar wrote: "We try to offer the service of a normal café but also to provide for those people who are unlikely to be welcome elsewhere. We hope that we are showing ways in which a café or bookshop could operate if their sole concern were not to be profit making."[99] Claudia explains that: "People could come in if they didn't have a lot of money,

[99] Centerprise Trust Ltd, 'Centerprise Annual Report 1978'.

Using the coffee bar as a place to meet, early 1990s. Copyright © Sherlee Mitchell.

because our food was very affordable, and they could just have a cup of tea and sit all day. So, because of that, and the safe nature, it ended up being called the mental health café. It was at the time of care in the community when people that might have been institutionalised were released into the community." One of these regular users, Desmond, is remembered by Janet Rees as an "extremely charming and intelligent and lively man, and a great big guy with huge Rasta hair, big hat. He was very imposing, and interested in us all, he was a bit of a philosopher." The coffee bar was popular with parents of small children, especially single mums, as Claudia describes because: "the babies could run back and forward and no one would say, 'Oh you can't do that' and 'You can't do this.' And it was very relaxed. Because it was such a relaxing place, sometimes people would look a bit put out if you had to say, 'Look, we're closing now.'"

The cost of food was kept deliberately low. One customer that Janet Rees describes, "Old Mac", used to collect his five pence for a cup of tea by walking along the road looking for halfpennies on the floor. She says "Old Mac was a good test of pricing, ambience, things like that, because it had to be the sort of place where Mac could come in with the dignity of having his five p for his cup of tea and legitimately occupy a space. You know, this wasn't a charity, it wasn't the Sally Army, you didn't have to sing a hymn in order to have your cup of tea, but you did have to have the five p."

Customers' behaviour could be challenging and it was not easy balancing the interests of very different people. Whether to ban customers was a regular agenda item at collective meetings but day-by-day workers had to deal with inappropriate behaviour themselves, as advice worker Wendy Pettifer describes: "When I was pregnant, I had a very big row with one of [the customers] when he kept flicking ash in this old guy's tea and I physically kicked him out, you know, picked him up and kicked him out. The door was made of reinforced glass. He came back to smash the door and really hurt his hand because I managed to lock him out."

Some customers were very vulnerable and could come to Centerprise in crisis. Jud Stone describes an especially harrowing incident:

> I remember being down in the coffee bar and suddenly this woman walks in from the street, totally naked. And the whole place, which was full of people, went silent. And she just walked across the room and sat down at a table and there was like ... "What?" and then people started talking again. And nobody looked at her. Nobody looked at her. And I think it was Dennis on shift.[100] And we said, "What are we gonna do?" And someone said, "Call the police." I said, "No, don't let's call the police." And he said, "I don't think I should go and talk to her. Why don't you go and talk to her?" So, I went and sat down and said, "Are you alright?"
>
> I don't know where she'd come from, but she'd walked up the whole of Kingsland Road, at that point. From Dalston, I think. And, she said, "They've taken everything from me, so I've taken my

[100] This incident is remembered differently by Robin Simpson, who recalls it being Jon Webber, an advice worker, who looked after the woman, not Dennis.

clothes off." I mean, she was clearly in a very kind of psychotic state. And Dennis went upstairs and got his coat and put it round her shoulders, in a very sort of tender and very sensitive way, and I think we kind of got her to go upstairs. I don't know what happened next, but actually, everyone coped. It was a stunning thing.

A regular customer enjoying a cup of tea, early 1990s. Copyright © Sherlee Mitchell.

Neil Martinson questions whether the project did enough for some of the coffee bar customers: "There was one guy who used to come in every evening, we called him Cheese Sandwich, right. He was a down-and-out and used to come in around six every evening. He'd have a cheese sandwich, and he would sit there till ten, and then he would go. And I've no idea where he'd go. He wouldn't say, he never talked, ever. Looking back on it, well, maybe we should have been thinking is there anything we could do to help the guy? Or maybe he didn't want any help; you can't assume that. And I think that was quite a big unmet need, but then, at the same time we couldn't do everything."

In the late 1980s with the closure of the GLC, it seemed likely that sources of funding for Centerprise would run dry, making the coffee bar profits more vital. The collective debated whether or not to take a more commercial approach but decided that to do so would "seriously affect the project's role as a community meeting place, a service that Centerprise is committed to provide."[101] This attitude was maintained into the 1990s, although small

[101] Centerprise Trust Ltd, 'Centerprise Annual Report 1986.'

The coffee bar with a view to the bookshop, early 1990s. Copyright © Sherlee Mitchell.

[102] Centerprise Trust Ltd, 'Centerprise Annual Report 1990.'

[103] Centerprise Trust Ltd, 'Centerprise Annual Report 1992', 1992, A Hackney Autobiography, Bishopsgate Institute.

measures, like restricting use of the chess set until after the lunch time rush, sought to ensure the café made a reasonable profit.[102] Claudia describes how the coffee bar made links with the Hackney Mental Health Consortium. By 1992 a Mental Health Vocational Training Project had been funded for four years, providing work experience to people with mental health issues in the coffee bar, and formalising somewhat the support that the coffee bar offered its customers.[103]

Preparing food in the Centerprise café, 1980s. Photograph courtesy of Maggie Hewitt.

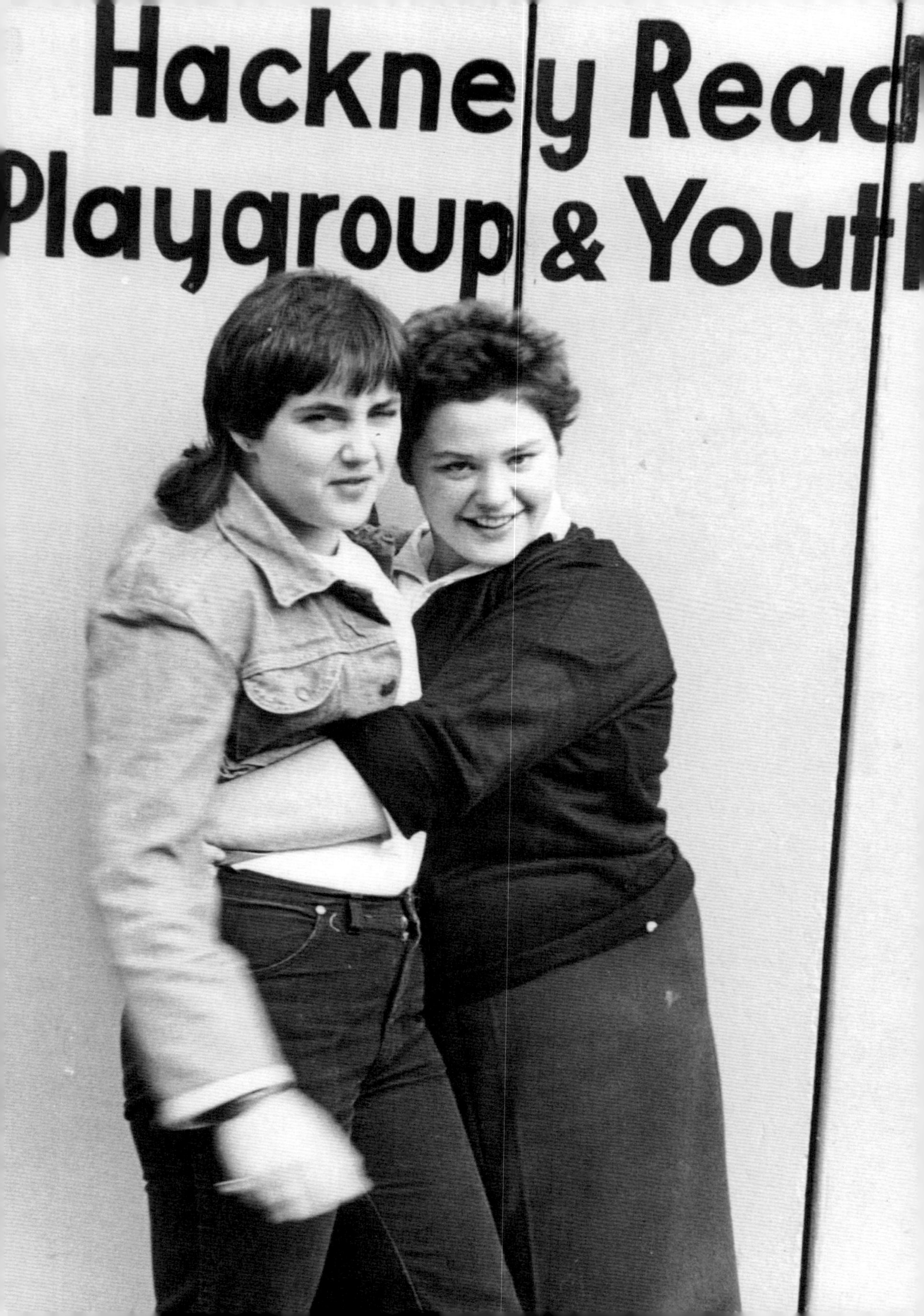
Hackney Read
Playgroup & Yout

The basement

Down beneath the coffee bar and bookshop, the basement was used for many purposes: the 136 playgroup, dances for more than a hundred people, classical, jazz and rock concerts, film shows and children's concerts.[104] There was a large meeting space, that, like the smaller rooms, could be booked at no charge. At one point, a small folk club met regularly for sedate and pleasant gatherings to hear a local singer and drink a couple of bottles of beer. In one of the rooms a cosy space gave young people somewhere of their own to hang out.

The 136 playgroup

The 136 playgroup was an independent group that based itself at Centerprise. They started to use one of the basement rooms in 1974, extending their hours after one year and were using both basement rooms by 1977.[105] They wrote in 1978: "We set out to provide a place for young children to play and mothers to meet, i.e. a playgroup. We soon discovered that playgroups are by necessity only really suited for certain kinds of families, and that what was really needed in this area was provision for the children of parents who have to work."[106]

Attempting to meet this need was a struggle as it was difficult to get the required funds to become a full-time nursery. The Centerprise basement was not ideal for a nursery because, as Larraine Worpole describes, it was used for other purposes in the evenings and the only outdoor space for the children to play in was a concrete yard.

Despite these obstacles in 1978 the playgroup reclassified themselves as a community nursery, had three full-time and two part-time members of staff, and had successfully campaigned with other community nurseries for parity of pay with Council-run nurseries. They were ready to move on from Centerprise, and were negotiating with the Council for their own premises.[107]

Youth

Oliver Flavin set up a youth space in the basement in 1975, equipping it "with table tennis, and a small area at the end which had bean cushions, chairs and a rug, a cupboard and a record player and bits and pieces like that." Beyond the basement, Centerprise aimed to involve young people in all aspects of the building. In 1982 they wrote: "by offering them a chance of participating in all aspects of the project, Centerprise offers its young users the opportunity

[104] Centerprise Trust Ltd, 'Report on the First Year's Work in the New Premises at 136 Kingsland High Street, London, E8. June 1974 – May 1975.'

[105] Centerprise Trust Ltd, 'Centerprise Annual Report 1978.'

[106] Ibid.

[107] Ibid.

Left: young customers of Centerprise outside the entrance, early 1980s. Photograph courtesy of Wendy Pettifer.

[108] Centerprise Trust Ltd, 'Centerprise Annual Report 1982.'

to take on responsibilities and gain some status not readily afforded in the outside world."[108] Young people used the bookshop and coffee bar extensively from the very beginning on Dalston Lane. They published writing, mounted exhibitions, attended classes at the reading centre, sought advice and attended events. There were holiday play schemes organised for young people, offering a combination of educational, creative and social activities and even group holidays that took them out of London.

Youth work was a major source of funding for Centerprise, but this money was not always used exactly as the grant-givers intended. Janet Rees describes how "we sort of mashed up the funding. ILEA used to fund us for youth work, and they were always wanting to see the youth workers. But we didn't have any youth workers, not when I was there. We all did a bit of youth work. So, we would have these jokes about showing the ILEA a bit of me and a bit of this person and a bit of that person."

Robin Simpson worked as a community and youth worker from 1974 to 1976. Although the youth aspect of his post was neglected somewhat in favour of developing the advice centre, he did organise summer play schemes and reading clubs in schools. While he developed good relationships with a few individual youngsters he was "a bit intimidated" by Hackney's youth as a group: "I had come straight from these ivory tower universities, I'd been six years at university, and I'd come from the provinces. So, London was still pretty overwhelming to me, after three years. … I was a bit straight-laced for the kids that used to hang out at Centerprise."

Oliver Flavin joined Centerprise in 1975, having taught in the borough and developed an interest in Caribbean literature through teaching African-Caribbean students. He hoped to make Centerprise more inclusive, for young people especially. At the time, it: "definitely wasn't the idea that you would go off and do your own thing … So, given that I was working with young people, it seemed to fit in, at least reasonably well, with the bookshop, the writing project, the coffee bar, and to some extent the literacy project." Oliver organised trips to the cinema or black bookshops like New Beacon Books. Over time he started to define himself more as a "Centerprise worker" than a "stereotypical youth worker … So, as time went on, I was less activities and more bookshop and writers' group." He worked closely with a group of young writers to produce a book of their poetry, *Talking Blues*. Writer Hugh Boatswain remembers that "we wanted to tell our stories from our point of view, we didn't want anyone else telling our stories."

Robin Simpson describes "a marvellous phase when the coffee bar became, astonishingly, a great centre for teenagers, mainly boys, to come and play chess. And, it became the rage among the young black lads in the area. So, you'd have this very paradoxical situation that, both the police and the Probation Service were very worried that we were a haven for truants, and they would come in expecting to witness scenes of vice and iniquity, and they'd find these lads playing chess together." Centerprise workers were conflicted about what to do about truants. They did not encourage school

Buildings have history

A punk band, The Vommets, playing in Centerprise's basement for the *Hackney People's Press* Christmas benefit, 1977. Children's drawings from the playgroup are visible on the back wall. Image courtesy of London Borough of Hackney Archives.

students to spend time there when they should have been at school, but equally they were reluctant to chase them away if it meant they moved on to less safe places.

Oliver remembers being criticised by a few people, who he says didn't really understand his job, for not being able to "sort out" a small group of young people who were using Centerprise as a place to hang out and sniff glue. He says "I didn't see how I was going to engage with them, because they didn't show any interest in me or what I was doing or the sorts of things I did with other kids." Eventually those youngsters grew up and moved on, but Centerprise's 1978 report describes a "continuing dilemma"; how to deal with young customers who could be "quite resistant as a group to anything organised on their behalf".[109]

[109] Centerprise Trust Ltd, 'Centerprise Annual Report 1978.'

Barbara Schulz, who first used Centerprise when bunking off school at fourteen, started going along to the Hackney Girls Project, which had started meeting in the basement in 1978. She remembers "just hanging out, talking, and having groups. It was somewhere to go rather than just sitting in the café bar, actually giving us some time and space."

The early 1980s saw a revival of organised youth activity, with youth workers Guy Farrar and Ric Mann placing a strong emphasis on young people taking ownership of the process themselves. They started a Young Photographers' Group for eleven to sixteen-year-olds which Barbara helped with

73

The Lime Green Mystery

Buildings have history

as "an older young person". Guy remembers them as a "real mish-mash of characters and dynamics".[110] Ric Mann describes how the young people would go out with their cameras and diligently develop their photographs themselves. The group made their own postcards, calendars, magazines and exhibitions for the coffee bar walls.

Hackney Unemployed Media Scheme (HUMS) catered for school leavers. Unemployment was high in Hackney in the 1980s, and young people were the worst off. In April 1981 29.2 per cent of sixteen to nineteen-year-olds in Hackney were unemployed, while the average rate for adult men was 18.3 per cent.[111] HUMS produced a magazine, *Starting Out*, and, through a connection to the Rio Cinema across the road produced tape-slides that were shown between films. They covered whatever the young people were concerned with and interested in, often political topics: revolutionary Nicaragua, the anti-nuclear protests at Greenham Common, deaths in custody.

Barbara explained that there would be weekly meetings run by the group's members:

> We'd take minutes, and think about what we wanted to cover. And then we'd divide the jobs up, who was going to do what. And then, we'd go out. We'd do storyboards, that was quite funny, we'd do little stories, and comic-strip stories. There was somebody that was an artist, some of us would do photography, some of us did the writing, some of us did the research, the layout. You know, we all took on different jobs, so we all felt we were part of the whole project.
> … Photography was always my thing, I was really into the photography side of it. I really liked layout and thinking about the organisation of a page, where you're going to put things, That was quite good. And just coming up with ideas and being able to negotiate with other people what we were going to cover each month, what were the issues of the time, what was important to us.

Ric describes the way the groups worked as radically different from anything the young people had experienced at school:

> The whole thing about sitting round as a group and talking about who we were and what we were doing, developing this ability to discuss our community, was a critical aspect of the whole thing, in a similar way to the publishing project upstairs. Those meetings were very much about developing a way of talking and discussing and relating to one another and developing a sense of community … we were using that space and that institution to explore the doing of community if you like. It was about doing what communities are about, becoming friends with one another, encouraging one another, listening to one another and giving each other a voice.

[110] Guy Farrar, conversation with Laura Mitchison, June 2015.

[111] Harrison, *Inside the Inner City*.

Previous spread: **Centerprise chess club. Copyright © Ken Worpole.**

Buildings have history

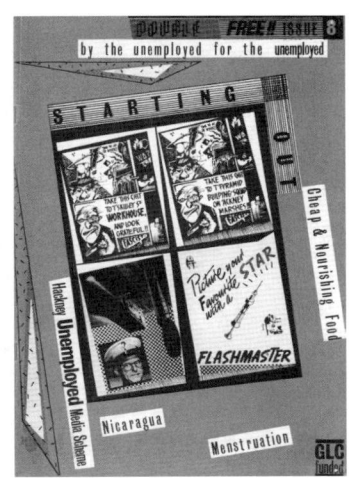

Above: front covers of *Inprint* and *Out of Focus*, both magazines produced by Centerprise Young Photographers' Group and *Starting Out*, a magazine produced by Hackney Unemployed Media Scheme.
Centre: postcard of a scene on Kingsland Road taken by a member of the Centerprise Young Photographers' Group. On the right another Young Photographer is aiming his camera off frame.
Below: postcard of a photograph taken by a member of the Centerprise Young Photographers' Group. All images courtesy of Guy Farrar, 1980s.

77

The Lime Green Mystery

The first floor

Back up the stairs, past the shops, you came to the first floor, with its rooms carpeted in hessian. Here you found a public office that housed a switchboard, electric typewriter and post boxes for scores of groups, two meeting rooms with tables and chairs and a small office for the advice centre, which would spill over into the other rooms during their busy drop-in sessions.

Offices and meeting rooms

Working in the Centerprise office, 1980s. Photograph courtesy Maggie Hewitt.

The public office was the reception area, information centre and the "general focus point for all workers".[112] Here someone needed to work every day to operate the switchboard, sort the mail and deal with enquiries. People would call Centerprise with all sorts of general questions, looking for welfare advice, or offering to volunteer. The office provided a typewriter, duplicator and photocopier for people to use at cost, along with post boxes held

[112] Centerprise Trust Ltd, 'Centerprise Annual Report 1986', 1986.

Left: an advice centre customer showing damage to clothing caused by damp, c. 1982. Photograph courtesy of Wendy Pettifer.

for all kinds of organisations. Hundreds of groups used Centerprise as their address at one time or another, including Hackney Against Cuts, punk group The Apostles, Theatre of Black Women and *An Phoblacht*, the newspaper of Sinn Fein.[113]

The only restriction on who could meet at Centerprise was made in 1973 when fascist groups were banned from meeting there.[114] Whether any ever attempted to do so is unclear and seems unlikely. It was hoped that the groups using the meeting rooms, free jazz enthusiasts, radical social workers and even the local Conservative Party, would make use of the other facilities on offer and connect with others. Not all the groups that met at Centerprise were sympathetic to the project's ethos, however, as these contrasting comments made in the workers' diary show:

"22 July 1971 – A meeting of the Clapton Communist Party which was extremely well attended by about 40 people, most of them staying on afterwards to have a chat about the project and the area".

"26 August 1971 – A meeting of the Dalston & Queensbridge Conservative Party. They were about 20 strong and took extremely little interest in the rest of the project, walking straight out without looking at the bookshop, walking straight through the coffee bar!"[115]

It wasn't only Tories who could be unfriendly. Ken Worpole describes some of the left-wing groups who used the meeting rooms upstairs "scowling" at the people working in the coffee bar "because they thought you'd sold out and weren't left-wing enough."

The facilities Centerprise offered were much more important in the pre-computer era as Janet Rees emphasises: "If anyone wanted to organise a meeting about something, start a campaign, what would they do? Well you'd come to Centerprise and you would use our equipment, that's what you'd do. And if you didn't have a Centerprise, then what would you do? You couldn't do it at all. You'd have to hand-write each poster."

The rooms on the first floor provided a base for independent organisations like Hackney Under Fives and Hackney Play Association, who moved into the new High Street premises and shared an office. Hackney Play Association existed to promote, through grassroots organisation and pressure on the local council, leisure and recreation activities for children, while Hackney Under Fives aimed to provide information for families with children under five and supported local nurseries and playgroups. They produced an *Under Fives Guide* listing all kinds of local services and facilities for small children, which was kept up to date and republished regularly. They advocated for more and better facilities for under fives and agitated for increased childcare provision for working parents, organising demonstrations such as one in 1977 that called for one thousand more nursery places in Hackney, part of a push for improvements in childcare across the country, closely connected to the women's liberation movement.[116]

Larraine Worpole worked for Hackney Under Fives as an outreach worker, and the most useful thing she did, she says, was working to improve

---

[113] 'Centerprise's Radical Mailboxes', *The Radical History of Hackney*, 17 August 2015, https://hackneyhistory.wordpress.com/2015/08/17/centerprises-radical-mail-mailboxes/.

[114] Taper, 'Report on the First Three Years'.

[115] Ibid.

[116] Centerprise Trust Ltd, 'Centerprise Annual Report 1978'; Hackney Flashers, 'Who's Holding the Baby? 1978', *Hackney Flashers: Work of a Women's Collective 1974–1980*, accessed 28 October 2016, https://hackneyflasherscollective-blog.files.wordpress.com/2013/05/the-state-provides2.jpg.

Design for Hackney Under Fives publicity, by Monica Strauss. Courtesy of Ken and Larraine Worpole.

conditions for families housed by the Council in bed and breakfast hotels in Finsbury Park. During this time the Under Fives' proximity to Centerprise's advice centre was especially useful.

As the office was up a narrow flight of stairs, Larraine remembers it as "not ideal" for people with young children to get to, but the benefits of being based in Centerprise were "what was around in that building". She says: "we were really pleased such a place existed. It housed everything we needed in a way." In 1978 Hackney Play Association wrote that the office space they shared with the Under Fives was "a mixed blessing". While they appreciated the easy access to the building's many resources, "working in such a busy building can be a strain: it is always difficult to do any quiet work because of the number of people who are constantly dropping in; the HPA office is used by Centerprise as a meeting room in the evenings, which means that work cannot be left out on desks. Being based in the same building, the work of the Play Association is often confused in the public eye with the work of Centerprise."[117] It is unclear how much longer the Play Association used their Centerprise office, but Hackney Under Fives stayed at Centerprise until 1992, when they closed down due to funding cuts.[118]

The advice centre

As Robin Simpson describes: "The area of advice wasn't tangible, whereas the bookshop, the literacy project, the coffee bar, all these things were all

[117] Centerprise Trust Ltd, 'Centerprise Annual Report 1978.'

[118] Centerprise Trust Ltd, 'Stop the Cuts at Centerprise Community Centre', c 1991, A Hackney Autobiography, Bishopsgate Institute.

obvious as soon as you walked through the door. In the meeting rooms, the actual advice work was in files and in my and the volunteer advisers' heads, and it was people coming through the door, it was part of our reputation."

When Robin started work, a few months before the move to the High Road, the advice centre was staffed by volunteers from Hackney Citizens Rights Group one night a week. Robin gently professionalised the service, saying he "tried to turn it into something a bit more permanent, six days a week, so that people could come in off the street and ask for help, we tried to have a more professional approach to keeping files and records and representing at tribunals."

The advice centre quickly amassed a bigger caseload than it could easily deal with, mainly problems to do with housing and benefits, then known as "the Social". Robin remembers: "some days coming in and seeing this huge stack of files, and all of them requiring letters. And I used to look at them and I'd think, oh the human misery that's represented in these papers, is just overwhelming." That was in the mid-seventies, before funding cuts and punitive reforms of housing and welfare legislation brought in by the Thatcher government. By the mid-1980s advice worker Sabina Bowler-Reed would tell PhD student Birgit Harris "If only we had more time, more staff, more money. If only the GLC was still with us, and there was no rate-capping, we could survive."[119]

In 1990 Centerprise estimated the advice centre had seen twelve hundred people the preceding year.[120] Their misery was not only contained in files. Centerprise worker Jean Milloy, describes people coming in with "creepy crawlies" in jars as evidence of the infestations that plagued their houses. Janet Rees, advice worker from 1979 to 1985 says: "We didn't offer any appointments, because we weren't capable of keeping to appointment times, so, if you wanted to see someone in the advice centre, you just had to queue up on Tuesday morning or Thursday evening for hours and hours. And so sometimes people wouldn't want to queue up again to check up what had been going on, so they'd call by in the hope of catching you on your way through. And of course, if you were there, you'd see them."

Waiting times may have been long, but at least there was a coffee bar and bookshop to spend time in while you queued. Pauline Brown, who first came into Centerprise to use the advice centre and continued to visit for many years, was happy with the way it worked: "I still continued going there if I've got complaints, there's always someone there I can really talk to ... And, I thought Centerprise was helping people quite well. Sometimes people said they may not get any help from there. But it depends on the cases individual people have, and what they could do and what they could not do, I introduced people there myself, say, 'Go to Centerprise and see what can be done.' You go in there, there's always going to be a lady downstairs, a man downstairs, like the reception, and they will direct you, and show you what area you should be going into."

Janet Rees explains how she "kept her head above water" by coordinat-

---

[119] Birgit Harris, 'The Federation of Worker Writers and Community Publishers – Gemeinde Arbeit Und Identitätsbildung' (unpublished PhD thesis, Oldenburg, 1986), 138, Bishopsgate Institute (A Hackney Autobiography).

[120] Centerprise Trust Ltd, 'Centerprise Annual Report 1990.'

Advice worker Carlynne Preville with customer, early 1990s. Copyright © Sherlee Mitchell.

ing a team of volunteers to work on the casework. These volunteers, from Hackney Citizens Rights Group, kept the centre going and were partly motivated, she thinks, by "wanting to be associated with Centerprise itself. The sort of funny old shabby glamour of the place really, and wanting to be part of that." Janet worked long hours, probably fifty-five or sixty a week when she first started, often fitting in home visits to view customers' disrepair problems on Sundays.

Janet describes how the collective pushed her, and the other advice centre staff, to collectivise issues and campaign. "There was no point in just doing casework because you could do it until the cows came home and it wouldn't make the slightest bit of difference. So, there was a lot of pressure on me, quite rightly, to do training and collective action and, make sure things got publicity so that we could make a difference further back in the decision-making process." Part of that was about providing information, through training and workshops and publications, so that people could gain the knowledge, skills and confidence to help themselves. Advice centre workers ran Workers' Educational Association classes on subjects like housing rights and social security benefits, which some of their customers attended to help themselves, their friends and neighbours. In 1978 Centerprise worked with the National Council for One Parent Families to produce the *Single Parents' Survival Guide to Hackney*, which was then given out free. Groups were formed with the intention of encouraging people to help each other and themselves. For instance, Janet recalls another advice worker, Lois

Pollock, starting a group for women to help each other stop their children being taken into care.

Janet remembers one time when a "collective" action was improvised by the advice workers themselves to take advantage of a media opportunity. She remembers her colleague, Lois, suddenly appearing on the six o'clock news after a group of Gypsies had arrived in Homerton:

> She just went down there. And the next thing I know, she's on the six o'clock news, and underneath her name it says, "Hackney Travellers' Support Group". She managed to get herself in front of the cameras and just invented this group on the spot. So, we had to create this group called Hackney Travellers' Support Group, which had already had its first television outing.
>
> There was a lot of fascist activity in Homerton at the time and it was not a good place for a group of Gypsies, because they were Gypsies rather than Travellers, to be. So, she just wanted to present another picture of the reaction of the people of Hackney.
>
> And we did a huge amount of work after that with Gypsies and Travellers, and they used to come into Centerprise, and the Hackney Travellers' Support Group had a really long life after that, and did a lot of good work with them. But it was just set up like that. There was an arrogance really, we knew that the media were very gullible, biddable, and that you could claim to be something and be it, and then fill in behind afterwards.

The piece of work Janet was most proud of was the Smalley Road Estate campaign, which was sparked by someone coming into the advice centre complaining of dampness in their brand new council housing: "It was heartbreaking, because the houses had only been up a year. So, I was incredibly surprised by this, mystified. And, I went up to see it, and sure enough, there was black mould all in a sort of line around all of the rooms that had an external face." Janet knocked on doors, discovered it was a common issue, got people in to do technical surveys and called together meetings of tenants. A group of fifteen tenants went together to the magistrate's court to file evidence of the dampness in their houses under the Public Health Act. They started to get publicity, three articles in the *Guardian*, a series in the *Architect's Journal* and a whole hour of television on the *London Programme*.

Janet recalls that finding out the problem was much more serious than they had initially thought:

> It cost them more to refurbish than it had to build it. And, what had happened was it was built with a design flaw, which is why the *Architects' Journal* was so interested in it, because here was a design right at the end of the 1970s where they thought they'd learnt all the lessons about systems building and flats, and knew that people wanted terraced houses and gardens, that's what could be done, and here it was being designed with this dreadful flaw. And then on

top of that the Direct Labour Organisation (DLO) in Hackney, which had built them and I wish I could say it was Bryant or, you know, one of the big builders, it wasn't, it was the Council's own DLO had filled the cavity walls with rubble rather than being bothered to carry it off site. Which is why the gable-end wall was so completely damp, because effectively there was no damp-proof course. There was a solid wall, because it was just full of rubble.

The campaign was a success. The tenants were moved out while the walls were taken apart, the rubble removed and the damp course restored, and then they got to return to their new homes, finally brought to a habitable state. However, Smalley Road was not the only place this had happened:

> And then of course it transpired, this was the third estate that they'd built with similar problems ... So by the time we did the *London Programme* we were able to drive them down this road where almost every property was empty, because, they knew that there was a problem. And even though they knew there was a problem with the design they hadn't owned up to it when we pointed out the problems in Smalley Road. And they'd continued to build, and continued to blame tenants for the dampness. It was dreadful, it really was. But, great fun to do, obviously it was an easy target.

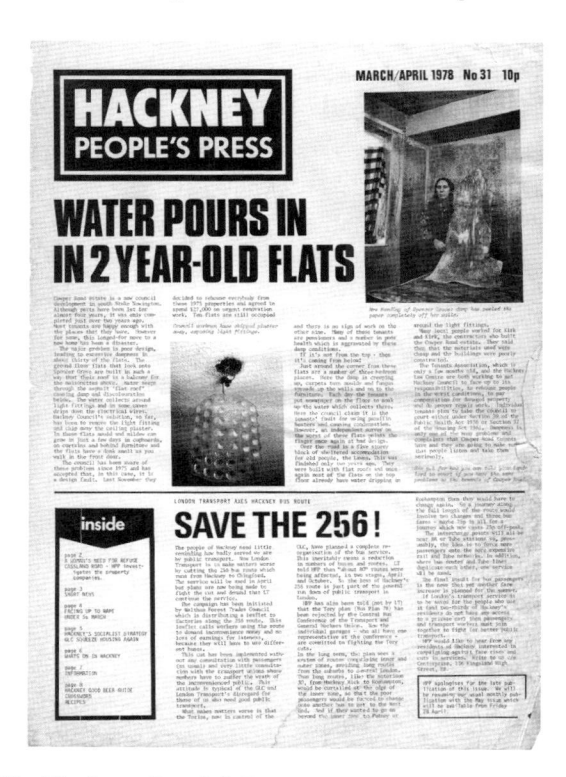

Front page of the *Hackney People's Press*, March /April 1978, No. 31.

The success of the Smalley Road campaign caused ripples that eventually overturned the Council's status quo: "The Council's architect lost his job as a result of it. I don't think he was sacked, but he was removed from his position. And, it caused tremendous ructions in the Council, and led to an overthrow of the old regime and its replacement by a more left-leaning, younger, less patrician group of Labour councillors, led by Anthony Kendall.[121] So, that was a peculiar outcome of all of that."

The campaign had a collective basis, Janet explains:

> we always encouraged people to work with other tenants, to find common cause, to go together down to the court to lay the information. And the fact that this had happened, and that the legal action had been successful, encouraged people to take legal action themselves. So, it was a great example. And also, some of the tenants from Smalley Road, if we did training on Section 99 they'd come and say, "Oh I did it, I stood there and this happened and that happened." So, we continued to use their knowledge and experience and expertise.

Wendy Pettifer describes how casework and campaigning was brought together in work around immigration and nationality, which expanded after the 1982 Nationality Act. During the 1980s community members were increasingly threatened with deportation under new, more stringent immigration controls.[122] Campaigns were launched to stop deportations, some of which Wendy helped to organise. In 1986 the deportation of Mrs Prem Lather, whose four children had been born in the UK, was stopped with Wendy's help.[123]

In keeping with Centerprise's traditional distrust of social work, Janet Rees explains they called "advice centre customers, customers, and that was a very deliberate and explicit thing to do. We didn't want to use the social services type terminology. We were very early adopters of something that local authorities adopted subsequently, which is this idea of treating users of services as customers." Janet even smoked cigarettes in an attempt to communicate better with her customers:

> I thought that the role of the advice centre was a bit like in those John Steinbeck books, you know, about communists working with people, you had to be on their side, delivering babies and all the rest of it, in order to win people around to the political viewpoint. And there was a bit of that going on in Centerprise I think. And it always struck me, that was part of the role of the advice centre. But one of the reasons I smoked was because, people were forever offering me cigarettes, and it felt really prim to say, "Oh no, I don't." So, I used to smoke.

Despite the advice centre's attempts to empower people by collectivising issues, changing the language used to describe them and providing training and resources to enable them to take action themselves, it was often an

---

[121] Anthony Kendall was a co-founder of Centerprise and established the advice centre. He remembers supporting the Smalley Road housing campaign as a Councillor.

[122] Centerprise Trust Ltd, 'Centerprise Annual Report 1982.'

[123] John Dillon, 'Victory for Family Facing Deportation', *Hackney Gazette*, 11 November 1986.

Two photographs from the publication *Breaking the Silence: Writing by Asian Women* showing school children campaigning against the deportation of the Hasbadak family in 1984. This family, originally from Turkey, were supported by a campaign based out of their children's school, William Patten Primary School in Stoke Newington. Copyright © Anna Sherwin.

authoritative voice on the end of the phone that made the difference, as Jean Milloy, who occasionally worked shifts in the advice centre, describes: "I discovered that if I phoned up the DSS and spoke to them, they would listen to me. If the tenant phoned up, they wouldn't. And that made me very angry. And this was me not knowing really what I was doing. … I was able to make a difference, but partly it was because of the way I sound, that I don't sound like a local person."

In 1996 the advice centre wrote "all too often we have had to 'pick up the pieces' as it were, after legislation that threatened or seriously eroded citizen's rights."[124] Over the years the advice centre adapted their tactics to suit ever-changing circumstances, as new legislation reduced the benefits available to people, council housing was sold off, the Poll Tax struggle caused an enormous rise in personal debt and immigration controls were tightened.

124 Centerprise Trust Ltd, 'Centerprise Annual Report 1996.'

Students helping themselves to cake at a book launch party for the reading centre publications: *I Got It Right*, *An Independent Woman*, *Doing My Flat Up* and *Giving Up Smoking*, 1983. Photograph courtesy of Maggie Hewitt.

Hackney Reading Centre

At the very top of the building the **Hackney Reading Centre** taught adults reading, writing and, later, numeracy in a small L-shaped room. The walls were covered in bookshelves and it was always a little untidy. At one end was an office, desks piled high with paper, in the middle were white **Formica** tables for students and teachers to sit around. In winter, it froze and everyone huddled around the gas fire, students and teachers keeping their hats and gloves on. On the wall above the fire was the student noticeboard, with students' writing pinned up. Before the classes started the teachers could hear the students coming all the way up the steep stairs. At break time, down they'd go again, to fetch tea and coffee from the coffee bar. Tutor **Jud Stone** muses: "Buildings have history. That building is very strong in my memory. All those rickety stairs and going up and up and up to the top floor to the reading centre."

When Sue Shrapnel started work at the reading centre in September 1975 she:

> walked into an empty room, absolutely empty, and that was extraordinary and very exciting in one way and totally spooky in another. And there were no books, there were no bookshelves, there was hardly any furniture. There was nothing on the walls. And so, all the things which are now features of a reading centre, like the students writing board over the fireplace, was an invention [we had to make].
>
> I remember interviewing [prospective students] and saying, "Well, as you see in this empty room, or relatively empty room, there's very little stuff you can give adults to read when they're learning. We write for each other" I used to say.[125]

Before coming to Centerprise, Sue had worked in the adult literacy movement, and been involved in the national literacy newspaper, *Write First Time*, which published student's writing. She found common cause with Glenn Thompson's original vision for Centerprise: "The push to create the reading centre at all was very much of a piece with the push to create the bookshop and the publishing project, and it was about access to print culture for people who hadn't got access to it. It was Glenn reading Paolo Freire and tripping out on that, thinking, this is what we want to do in east London, that was one of the strong motivations behind the negotiation that got the reading centre established."[126]

The scarcity of literacy provision at the time locally is demonstrated by the fact that in the 1970s the reading centre had the only full-time literacy tutor in Hackney.[127] In 1975, just as the reading centre was beginning, a national

[125] Shrapnel, Interview with Sue Shrapnel (later Gardener) by Maggie Hewitt.

[126] Ibid.

[127] Centerprise Trust Ltd, 'Centerprise Annual Report 1978.'

campaign tried to improve adult literacy provision. The campaign was launched by a BBC Television series watched by millions of viewers called *On the Move*, about a removal man, played by Bob Hoskins, who could not read. Despite this, adult literacy students remained "a forgotten group" according to Irene Schwab, who worked at the reading centre from 1981 to 1990. She says that literacy classes were not organised according to a national standard: there was no set curriculum, no qualifications to work towards, no exams. This gave Sue, in her empty room, considerable freedom and she began using the language experience approach to teaching adults to read. This used the student's own words to teach them to read, the idea being that these would be more easily recognised by the student and that students would feel that their experiences were being validated. Richard Gray, who taught an outreach literacy class for the reading centre to people living in supported housing provided by Peter Bedford Housing Association, explains how he used the method:

> We'd talk for five or ten or fifteen minutes about a journey they wanted to go on, or a shopping trip they wanted. Something which mattered to them. And I'd write it down, and choose one of the sentences that they had said, and we would then read it several times, go over it and over it and over it, so that they could say it back to me.
>
> And then I'd take the sentence as written on a strip of paper, on a cut strip, and just, point to the words, so that you associate the shape on the page with the word that you've said.
>
> And when you could do it on the whole strip, then you cut the words, so you've got separate words and you make it like a jigsaw puzzle. And put them together in order. And that's how you build up this kind of confidence of reading.

Writing was made easier to read by line breaking, as the introduction to a reading centre publication, *Every Birth It Comes Different* explains:

> Some of the pieces
> are written in short lines.
> Each line corresponds
> to a unit of meaning.
> They are not poems.
> We often print writing like this
> to make it easier to read.
> We call it line breaking.[128]

In January 1984 over 70 per cent of reading centre students were from Caribbean countries, while many had been born in the UK to parents from the Caribbean.[129] The number of students steadily grew; there were fifty in 1978, sixty in 1983 and eighty-two in 1986, around half of whom attended several times a week.[130] The small size of the room restricted the centre from expanding any further.

---

[128] Hackney Reading Centre, *Every Birth It Comes Different: Writings from Hackney Reading Centre*, 1980.

[129] Irene Schwab and Jud Stone, *Language, Writing and Publishing: Work with Afro-Caribbean Students* (Hackney Reading Centre – City and East London College, 1985).

[130] Centerprise Trust Ltd, 'Centerprise Annual Report 1978'; Centerprise Trust Ltd, 'Centerprise Annual Report 1983'; Centerprise Trust Ltd, 'Centerprise Annual Report 1986.'

In the 1970s the teaching was done mainly in pairs made up of students and trained volunteers, with students sharing their work at the end of sessions. There was considerable pressure to recruit and train volunteers to meet the demand, and significant challenges in finding the right people for such "a complex and delicate teaching job".[131] Jud Stone, who taught at the centre in the 1970s and 1980s, remembers "we didn't want do-gooders". Irene Schwab, who in 1981 took over from Sue Shrapnel, instigated some changes in the teaching techniques, reducing one-on-one work with volunteers and increasing group work. This, Jean Milloy, who taught in the 1980s, describes as "a political decision, that people learned better in groups than one-to-one".

Irene describes how writing was pinned on the board above the gas fire[132] and shared with other students: "Our administrative worker would type up some of the work that they had written, and we'd have the work on the walls, and students would come and read what other students had written. And they might write a response, and that would go up too. And that was one of the ways in which we decided on things like what books we would publish. So, if somebody wrote something that interested other people, then we'd think about that as potential for publishing. And then if there were things we wanted to publish, we'd ask everybody to read them and comment on them and so on."

Students' books ranged from short simple beginner readers, like *Giving Up Smoking* (1983) by Dawn Brown, to extensive autobiographies like *Pure Running* (1982) by Louise Shore. Publishing students' writing normally involved the student/writer working closely with one or more of the tutors to prepare the text from work they had first done in class. The most complex publication produced by the reading centre was *Every Birth It Comes Different* (1980), a collection of writing about birth involving a group of student/writers. The idea of the book began when Shirley Elliot, a student, wrote an account of her son's birth which inspired others to do the same. Liesbeth says:

> It just meant lots and lots of talking in the groups, and reading each other's work, and, thinking about different customs. And also, it linked into debates around men's control of childbirth, having to go into hospital to give birth ... It was part of the feminist movement to take control of your bodies and take control over birth ... actually the students did [often] wanted to have hospital births. So, it was an interesting debate going on at that time.
>
> Then we also had to make a decision about whether it was only going to be women's writing or whether there were going to be men writing about their experiences of women giving birth, and we decided [to publish both], because there were some good pieces that had been written by men. And I'm glad we did that actually. Because it also widened the discussion, you know, within the group ... Men would say things and women would shout them down. One

[131] Centerprise Trust Ltd, 'Centerprise Annual Report 1978.'

[132] In *Language Writing and Publishing* (1985) Irene Schwab and Jud Stone write that "it is worth mentioning that the writing board is situated above the gas fire where people come to stand and get warm so it is a focal point of the room physically as well as ideologically!" (p.26)

or two men were very rigid about what their place was, their place was not to be there. And at that time, the women's movement were saying, well men should be at the birth. But the men were saying, "Well it's nothing to do with me and we don't want to have anything ..." And the women were saying, "Aagh!" you know. "We're doing it; you can bloody see it, you suffer too," kind of thing, "You get the joy too."

After the first two years the reading centre was not able to pay tutors to work on publishing. Nevertheless, the tutors continued to work with students turning their writing into books in their spare time. While this meant extra work, it could be a labour of love, as Jud remembers:

Oh, [publishing was] such fun – that was interesting in the [history project] meeting when I said, "It was such fun," and Liesbeth said it was very hard. And I think, yeah, it was, but actually I love that way of everything being involved. It was all part of a sort of a seamless kind of thing with my life, because it sort of worked all together somehow.

How do you mean?

Well, because in order to do those books, we did so much more work and then we'd do it in each other's houses. I mean, that's how people became friends as well. Liesbeth became a friend. Still is. And I can remember sitting in her garden discussing what we were doing and how we were doing it, and then when Irene and I were pasting-up in the commune on our big table.

But I suppose I like that combination of creating things that are tangible as well as working with the people and then all the meetings we had with all the people to discuss it all and all those photos from the photo agencies that we had and choosing which ones to put in and which ones not. And how proud people were of their books. And how the launches were such great parties and people brought all these cakes and food, all this variety of food, and did readings. And, people actually stood up in front of people to read, and that's like really having a voice and the confidence to stand up and read your work.

The classes, Liesbeth remembers were partly a "help place" for the students who would bring in letters they needed to read or write. There was a strong focus on gaining functional literacy skills. Liesbeth says:

We did a lot of work on form-filling, because there were a lot of forms to be filled in, as there always are. Working in adult literacy, it is amazing the strategies that people have to not expose their lack of literacy skills, how functioning they are in society, but how terrified they are. I had one student who was a young Irish guy who had come over to work on the building sites. A building site would be, say, twenty minutes from where he was staying, but he would do a route of an hour and a half to get there, because that was the route that he knew, he couldn't read any of the Underground signs. So we'd [teach] travelling on the transport, learning place names, learning Underground signs. I mean very basic stuff, a lot of it, survival stuff. So all this publishing sounds all very good, and it's exciting and it's fantastic, but actually it's interesting that I'd totally forgotten about the amount of absolutely basic literacy that you needed. And then also the next stage of writing letters home. People didn't make international calls then, it was expensive. So, written communication was important.

Students came to the reading centre because in some way they had been failed by the education they had received as children; they might have been "school phobic" or had missed out on school due to caring responsibilities, bullying or racism. Jean Milloy says:

> I remember working with students in the reading centre who had had the sort of education in the Caribbean that was sent out from England. So they'd been reading Wordsworth, about the daffodils. And they were sent pictures of daffs. I mean that was all fascinating. And it all became part of talking, and thinking about, you know, why were people having to come to classes, why were mature adults, who were perfectly in control of their lives, why were they having to come to classes to learn to read? And why were children coming out of school not being able to read adequately?[133]

Some came to the reading centre because it was convenient, others because they appreciated the informality and that little in the untidy room reminded them of school. Where possible students were encouraged to go on to more formal courses at colleges, and the reading centre ran a College Links course to help ease the progression.

Liesbeth remembers that some students easily improved but others "just couldn't. Either they had learning difficulties that at that time weren't recognised or psychological blockage, or fear. I mean people would come to classes shaking, literally shaking with fear." Liesbeth describes how "it could be very, very frustrating, and worrying when you're working with a student who, you know from their life story is a really intelligent person, and you can't get to grips with, why can't this person learn to read? It's really, really frustrating, and really horrible. Because, you feel you should be able to help them through it." With these obstacles to overcome, improving literacy as an adult was often a long term commitment. Julia Clarke, a former tutor at the reading centre, concluded in a report written in 1989: "Adult Basic Education teaching has evolved a style which accommodates people who learn slowly for whatever reason."[134] Many students attended classes over several years. At a discussion amongst reading centre coordinators held in 1980 one of the participants concluded that it was not simply about learning skills as "writing

---

133 The 1978 Centerprise Annual Report describes how some school children enquired about coming to classes; the youngest to do so, shockingly, was ten years old. The reading centre could only take adult students.

134 Julia Clarke, "'This Is a Lifetime Thing'. Outcomes for Adult Basic Education Students from Hackney Adult Education Institute and the Hackney Reading Centre." (ALFA (Access to Learning for Adults): The North & East London Open College Network, June 1989), A Hackney Autobiography, Bishopsgate Institute.

The Lime Green Mystery

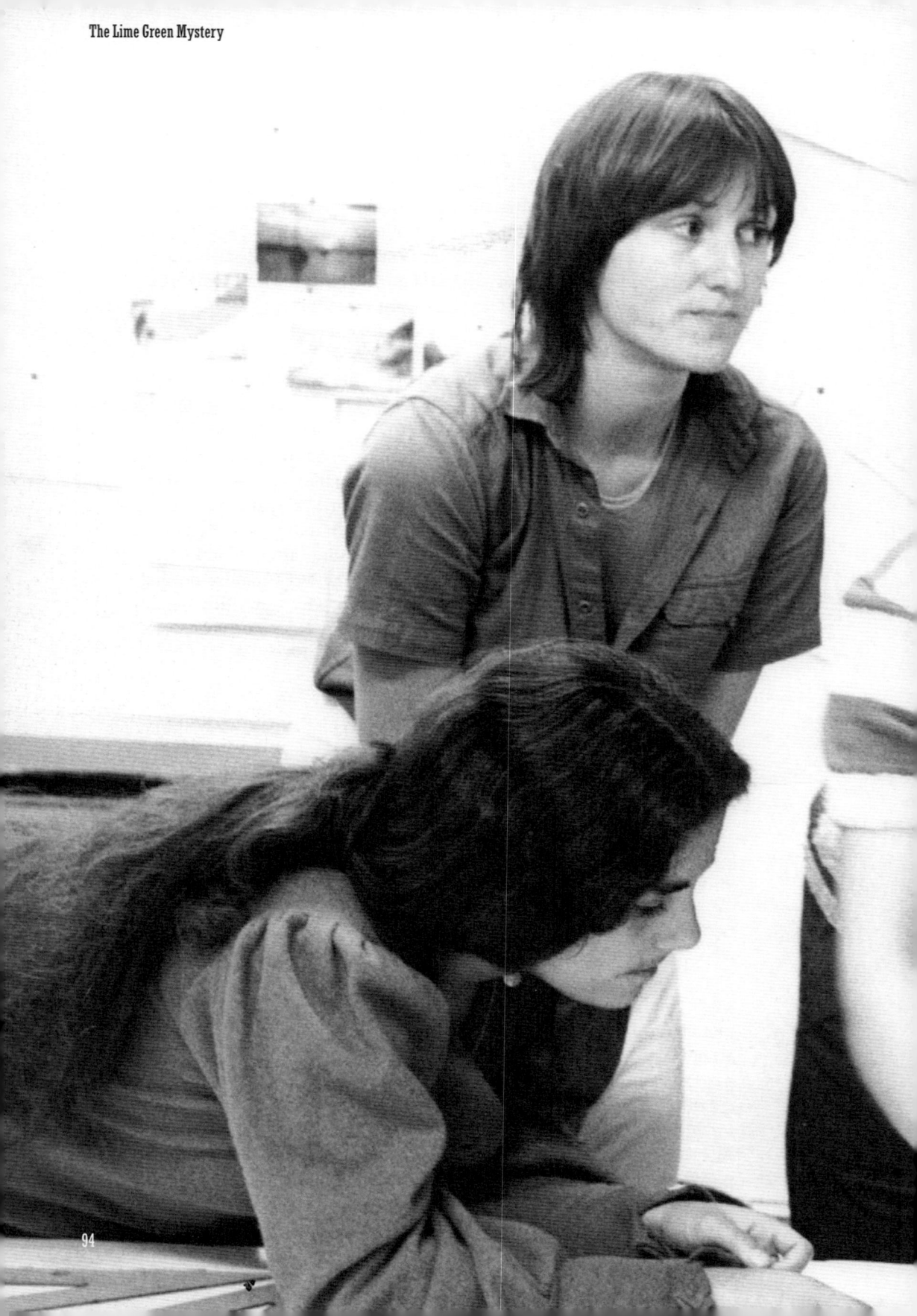

Buildings have history

and reading is to do with thoughts and thinking and speaking. And it's so tied up with the way people see themselves ... in the world and their section of the world or community. It's important to keep the complexity of it in mind because otherwise you get frustrated that people aren't doing whatever it is you think they should be doing, or could be doing, or it would be good for them to do."[135]

[135] 'Extracts from a Transcript of Hackney Reading Centre Co-Ordinator's Discussion of Aims, Objectives and Priorities', n.d., A Hackney Autobiography, Bishopsgate Institute.

Tutor Chris O'Mahony describes friendships with some of her students that developed despite their very different belief systems: "Ethel was terribly worried about my lack of religion, I do remember that, and she and some of the other older ladies were always trying to get me to go to church with them. And eventually, I got exasperated and said, 'Okay Ethel, look, when we die, you'll go to Heaven and I'll go to Hell. And you can look down and laugh at me, okay, and that'll be fine.' And she said, 'I wouldn't want to go without you Chris.' And I was so struck, and I thought, actually, she's got a point, you know, because if you do believe in it, and you really, really want to be with the people you love, you are going to want them to be in Heaven with you. So I was a bit more tolerant about them trying to convert me after that."

Jud notes that "the students talked to each other, so there's a whole range of stuff goes on that isn't mediated by us [the volunteers and staff]." Chris remembers the efforts students made "to do very sweet things at Christmas, they all used to bring food in to share with us, and they used to sort of, vie with each other for the best jerk chicken or the best goat curry or this, that and the other. Oh, and the Jamaican Christmas cake, oh my God. Oh! To die for." Relationships developed during trips to the seaside, Kew Gardens, the Commonwealth Institute and an annual writing weekend held at Ruskin College, Oxford which Jean Milloy remembers: "was part of the process of saying to students, you are students, this is a university."

Some expeditions fitted especially well into the Freirean approach to education as integral to political struggle, as well as being fun. Chris recalls an especially memorable trip to the women's peace camp at Greenham Common, where the students joined in with invading the military base:

> It was just a hoot, it really was great. We hired a minibus, and it was probably the worst minibus in the world. It went so slow. Everyone else was heading to Greenham, it was a massive demonstration day. And Irene was driving, and all these busloads of women were passing us, and all our women were going, "Put your foot down Irene, put your foot down!" She was going, "I've got it on the floor!" And we were still chugging along at forty miles an hour on the motorway.
>
> Anyway, eventually we got there. And, you know, they probably were the first black women that had been seen at Greenham. So,

Previous spread: reading centre workers laying out *Every Birth It Comes Different*. **From left to right: Aydin Mehmet Ali, Liesbeth de Block, Sue Shrapnel and Jud Stone, c. 1979. Photograph courtesy of Jud Stone.**

At work in the reading centre, 1980s. Photograph courtesy of Maggie Hewitt.

all these kind of hippie-dippy dykes came rushing out to embrace them and welcome them going, "Oh, do you know, it's amazing you're here, it's so fantastic you've come." And they're hugging and kissing them and everything. And [the students are] all a bit sort of, taken aback at this very effusive welcome, all these white women.

Anyway, [the students] were passing the rum around. It was one of those "hold hands around the base" events. Everyone whispered to everyone else to go silent, and you could see the police and the soldiers all getting really really scared, the silence was much more terrifying for them than the noise and the screaming that had been going on before. There were thousands upon thousands of women there.

And, we all held hands around the base, and suddenly these bolt cutters come out, and they're being passed from hand to hand. So some of our women just used them, cut holes in the fence. And the next thing we know, all the fences are coming down, and, we're inside the base. And my kids had been really anxious about me going, because there'd been a lot of stuff on the news about it, "Don't get arrested, don't get arrested." And I'm thinking, "Oh God, they'll really kill me if I get arrested." Anyway, we got pushed inside. And I got stuck, because my feet got tangled up in some barbed wire, onto which, a piece of corrugated iron landed on top of my feet, tangled in the barbed wire. So I was stuck inside the base when

Top: **Sue Shrapnel using the typewriter in Hackney Reading Centre, 1970s. Photograph courtesy of Jud Stone.**
Bottom: a book launch party for the reading centre publications: *I Got It Right*, *An Independent Woman*, *Doing My Flat Up* and *Giving Up Smoking*, 1983. Photograph courtesy of Maggie Hewitt.
Right: typed piece of writing from student Ruby Moran to tutor Julia Clarke, November 1981. Courtesy of Julia Clarke.

"Ruby's view of Julia" by Ruby Moran

Ruby's view of Julia

She tall.
She have different colour hair.
She have her hair in a fringe.
She have on thick lenses, with blue eyes.
She have big feet. She wear size 8½
so she's a big woman.
She have three children and she work very hard.
And she is a good mother.
I don't know how she cope with them some of the time
because they are little devils
according to what she said.
She get upset sometime when they give her trouble.
She works at home and she has to work here,
but still she carry out the motherhood way.
She have to, they belongs to her.
She likes to smoke roll ups. Very bad.
Still, she has to smoke, she got too much on her plate.
She have a good husband.
He helps with the kids as well.
He babysits when she come here.
When six o'clock come she has to hurry back to go and relieve him,
I guess by then he have enough.
She's quite nice, I know her quite a while now, I like her.
I give her 8 out of 10.
So keep up the good work Mum!

November 1981

The Lime Green Mystery

A book launch party, 1983. Photograph courtesy of Maggie Hewitt.

there was a push back, and everybody kind of went back the other way, leaving me stranded.

And I was really shitting myself. Now one of the women came and got me actually, she came and wrestled this piece of corrugated iron off my feet and untangled me and dragged me out again. So

> thanks to her I didn't get arrested. But we had such a good day out, they talked about it for forever afterwards, it was one of their best things ever.

By the time Irene and Jean were leaving the reading centre in 1990 to go on to other things, adult education was changing. By now literacy classes were much more widely available. Jean describes a "push for qualifications" and new concern with accountability. In 1990 the loss of the ILEA was troubling. From its inception the ILEA had funded the reading centre via City and East London College, and run projects like the Afro-Caribbean Language and Literacy Project, which connected the centre with others doing similar work and provided a forum to share their developing expertise more broadly. The reading centre continued in the next decade, now with the support of Hackney Community College, but over time it became increasingly precarious and relied more heavily on volunteers.

The Lime Green Mystery

Publishing project office. Image courtesy of London Borough of Hackney Archives.

The publishing project

Next door to the reading centre was the publishing project's office, a dim, attic-like room. The walls were lined with boxes of books and cassette tapes. Oral history interviews were played on the tape deck as the transcripts were laboriously typed out word for word. In tea breaks publishing worker Ken Worpole would swap the cassette for Miles Davis. In this room writers and editors pored over manuscripts, and in the evenings writing groups met. Writer and oral historian Roger Mills remembers going to the "A People's Autobiography of Hackney" group meeting on Wednesday nights, when it always seemed to rain: "I can never remember going to a meeting where it wasn't chucking it down with rain outside. And, we'd sit in chairs in their top room with buckets around the floor, which were taking in the drips from the ceiling."

Publishing at Centerprise started in 1972, when Centerprise was on Dalston Lane. Ken Worpole, then an English teacher at Hackney Downs School, experienced the scarcity of books that his students could relate to their own lives as "a major frustration."[136] With another teacher, John Bowler, Ken produced a reading book for his students set in Hackney, illustrated with photographs of local children, some of whom were African-Caribbean, which was then very unusual. He approached Centerprise with the book and *Hackney Half-Term Adventure* was published in the spring of 1972.

The next book Centerprise produced also came from Hackney Downs School; the *Poems* of student Vivian Usherwood. Vivian was twelve years old, African-Caribbean, lived in care homes and was taught by Ken Worpole and Ann Pettit. Margaret Gosley remembers when she first saw Vivian's poetry: "Ann Pettit came in to the library with this bunch of papers and said, 'I've got this little boy in my class,' she said, 'he's such a handful, he's lovely, but he's up and down and bouncing around the whole time. And the only way I can calm him down is to say "Go and sit on the windowsill and write a poem, Vivian"'. And she said, 'I've got this bunch of poems, and some of them are lovely.'"

With some help from Ann, Ken, Glenn and Margaret, Vivian produced his book *Poems*, which was first duplicated and then printed by Centerprise in 1972. Vivian's poetry is often poignant and sad, detailing how he felt rejected in his care home and at school, although some, like "The sun glitters when you look up" describe an irrepressible beauty found in everyday life. They sold better than many better known works of poetry and within two months the first edition of five hundred copies had sold out. By the end of March 1979, 8,112 copies had been sold with eight hundred sent to the Swedish Workers' Educational Association.[137]

That same year, 1972, for Hackney National Union of Teacher's centenary,

[136] Worpole, *Local Publishing & Local Culture*, 3.

[137] Centerprise Trust Ltd, 'Centerprise Annual Report 1978'.

The Lime Green Mystery

To promote his book Vivian Usherwood appeared on a Saturday night television programme and set his poems to piano music played by a fellow student, Philip Ramocon (later a professional musician). Margaret Gosley says fame did not go to Vivian's head: "Really he wanted to be a martial arts fiend. He had no delusions of grandeur, at all." Tragically Vivian died in 1980 in a house fire in Stoke Newington, aged nineteen.

Above: four school students from Hackney Downs appear on BBC2 Saturday night arts programme, *Full House*, December 1972. Philip Ramocon at the piano, poets (from left to right): Tom Murphy, Danny Morfett and Vivian Usherwood. Presenter Joe Melia sitting on the platform. Photograph supplied by BBC to Ken Worpole.

Right: (top) front and back cover of Vivian Usherwood's *Poems*, published by Centerprise, 1972. Cover photograph copyright © Neil Martinson and (bottom) section of page showing 'The Sun Glitters As You Look Up'.

Initially *Poems* was duplicated but shown here is the later printed version.

Our other publications include:

'If it wasn't for the houses in between...' A collection of social and historical documents about Hackney, including maps and photos. 60p

'A Hoxton Childhood' An autobiographical account of a working-class childhood in this well known district of the East End. 50p

'Hackney Half Term Adventure' A community-based reading book for children, illustrated with many photographs. 20p

'Christine Gillies: Poems' A collection of poems by a young woman. 10p

'Roger Coles' A collection of poems by a sixteen year old school boy. 5p

'When I was a Child' The childhood autobiography of a dressmaker, set in Hackney 1899-1913. 15p

'At the Cliff's Edge' An illustrated pirate story written by a local boy of thirteen. 25p

'Rabbit Island' An illustrated fantasy story for children written by a local girl. 20p

'The Autobiography of a Hackney Shoe-Maker' Provisional title: a detailed autobiography covering life and work in Hackney 1901-1966. Available end of December.

Published by Centerprise
66a Dalston Lane London E8 01-254 1620

Vivian Usherwood Poems

10p

The Sun Glitters As You Look Up

The sun glitters, is shining bright!
The sky is blue!
The clouds are no longer there:
It glitters as I look up!
Bright, it is bright as my sister's face:
The sun looks like a face without a body,
Just round, with a nose and two eyes.
If only that beautiful face would come down-
It will be mine,
And I shall shine with it.
As dim as I am now I will be brighter,
Even brighter than the sun itself.
So it shall be,
And I shall be as dim as ever,
For it shall stay there for many years to come.

Ken worked with another fellow teacher, Richard Whitmore, to publish a "Jackdaw-type collection of local history materials, with an emphasis on the social history of the borough. A collection of maps, facsimile posters, extracts from books about Hackney, transcripts of tapes made with elderly Hackney people about their school-days, photographs and so on, called '*If it wasn't for the houses in between*' ... The interest this aroused, especially in bringing forth elderly people who had written about their lives, made us realise that local history, particularly the social history of the last hundred years, was a very activating subject to study, promoting quite the opposite of that 'apathy' which was supposed to be a 'condition of life' in the teaching of school history."[138] An "astonishing" 2,250 copies of the pack were sold within ten months.[139]

To further develop this study of the area's social history, an oral history group started in September 1972, "A People's Autobiography of Hackney". Inspired by an "extraordinarily chaotic conference at Ruskin College, Oxford, in May of 1972 ... called a 'History Workshop'", the group aimed to "make history an engaged mass activity".[140] The group was convened as a Hackney Workers' Educational Association (WEA) class by Ken Worpole and involved both young and old members. Through its work interviewing and publishing the memoirs of older people in the borough the group encouraged more local, older and working class readers through the doors of the bookshop to buy the autobiographies and works of local history they produced.

The success of these early ventures encouraged Centerprise to establish a dedicated publishing project, which Ken Worpole left his teaching post in 1973 to staff full-time. The project hoped to foster a local culture of writing and publishing, working in tandem with the bookshop. In 1975 Centerprise wrote that "publishing books by local writers ... has greatly widened the range of people who use the bookshop, to the point where we think that local publishing should be an essential part of the service that a community bookshop offers, for in our experience local publishing has been an enormous factor in breaking down the mystique attached to books and bookshops."[141]

Almost as soon as Ken started work, local people started bringing him manuscripts, and the resulting quick succession of local books created a conversation, with some texts penned in direct response to ones that had gone before. One of the authors, taxi driver Ron Barnes, wrote in the introduction to his first book *A Licence to Live*: "If you enjoy this story I hope it will encourage you to write your own; if you don't enjoy it then at least it will be a guide to you on how not to write your story."[142] The project inspired interest and recognition from outside Hackney, in 1974 winning the Young Publishers Award in recognition of its "innovatory work".[143] Between 1972 and 1993, when the publishing project came to an end, at least ninety-four books were published at Centerprise.[144]

Having both a publishing project and bookshop under the same roof solved the distribution problem that plagued many community publishers.

---

[138] Worpole, *Local Publishing & Local Culture*, 4.

[139] Worpole, 'About Hackney: Community Publishing at Centerprise.'

[140] Worpole, *Local Publishing & Local Culture*, 9.

[141] Centerprise Trust Ltd, 'Report on the First Year's Work in the New Premises at 136 Kingsland High Street, London, E8. June 1974–May 1975.'

[142] Ron Barnes, *A Licence to Live: Scenes from a Post-War Working Life in Hackney* (London: Hackney Workers' Educational Association: Hackney Libraries Committee; Distributed by Centerprise, 1974), II.

[143] Centerprise Trust Ltd, 'Report on the First Year's Work in the New Premises at 136 Kingsland High Street, London, E8. June 1974–May 1975.'

[144] This number is based on the list of publications compiled by the project A Hackney Autobiography: Remembering Centerprise, which at the time of writing is not definitive.

The locally produced books often sold in runs of thousands, vastly outselling the other books on offer in the bookshop, even national best-sellers. Centerprise books were also sold through a network of twenty local newsagents. An early publication, Dot Starn's *When I Was a Child* (1973), about growing up in Hackney around the turn of the century, sold one thousand copies in three months. Ken Worpole wrote that "between March 1976 and February 1977 we sold 6,922 of our local history titles in Hackney alone."[145] All these sales meant that in the 1970s the project made a considerable surplus that could be invested back into Centerprise. For instance, in 1977 publishing's surplus was £7,417, less than the bookshop at £11,502 but more than the coffee bar at £3,235.[146]

Bookshop and publishing workers tended to collaborate, sharing ideas and expertise. Maggie Hewitt joined Centerprise as a publishing worker in 1979, having first taught for fifteen years, most recently as head of English at a Newham school. There she had taught many Asian students, and so was able to introduce books for children in Hindi, Punjabi and Gujarati into the shop. In her report to the collective after three months in post, Maggie wrote that there had been a "definite response" to the books already, and that she was now recommending books for the education section.[147] Both bookshop workers and publishing workers like Maggie would write book reviews, for instance for Rosemary Stone's anti-racist *Children's Book Bulletin*.

Maggie remembers how part of her work involved encouraging people to write: "We were trying to get into more schools, to encourage the young people to see themselves as writers. And I did an exhibition about, what is a writer? So, I remember I would go into schools and say 'Well, what do you think a writer looks like?' you know, and they all said, 'They're men. They're white. They're old and they have white beards.' And then I'd say, 'Well, have a look at this,' and show a photo of Vivian Usherwood, you know, and I said, 'Well he's written a book, and this is his book.'"

The main forms of literature published in 1975 were "writing by children, local autobiographies of working class life, local history materials and individual collections of poetry."[148] Over time the books published became more ambitious in terms of content, size and process. 1975 saw the publication of *The Gates*, an autobiographical novel written by two "school phobic" teenagers. "A People's Autobiography of Hackney" began to publish larger, more complex works of local history, the first of which brought together local people's memories in *The Threepenny Doctor: Dr Jelley of Hackney* (1974).

The eccentric Dr Jelley, who practised medicine in Hackney from 1911, was well remembered locally for his top hat, cheap fees and tendency to prescribe steak to his patients instead of expensive tonics. Through the figure of Dr Jelley the group documented life before the National Health Service and the legalisation of abortion, an age when basic medical care and contraception were out of reach for most ordinary people. Group member and historian Anna Davin recalls how Dr Jelley:

---

[145] Worpole, *Local Publishing & Local Culture*, 18.

[146] Centerprise Trust Ltd, 'Centerprise Annual Report 1978.'

[147] Maggie Hewitt, 'Maggie's Three Month Review', March 1979, A Hackney Autobiography, Bishopsgate Institute.

[148] Centerprise Trust Ltd, 'Report on the First Year's Work in the New Premises at 136 Kingsland High Street, London, E8. June 1974–May 1975.'

If It Wasn't for the Houses Inbetween, a collection of local social history resources. Published by Centerprise in 1972.

The Interview by Roger Mills, a short story about a visit to the Labour Exchange as a young school leaver. Adapted by **Sue Shrapnel** and **Ken Worpole** for beginner readers and illustrated by **Alan Gilby**. Published by Centerprise in 1976.

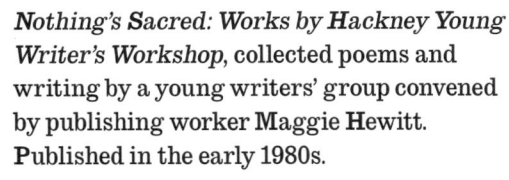

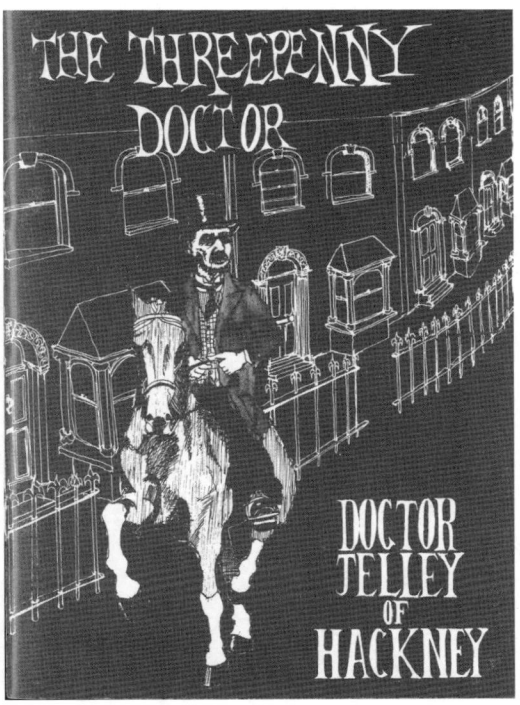

Nothing's Sacred: Works by Hackney Young Writer's Workshop, collected poems and writing by a young writers' group convened by publishing worker Maggie Hewitt. Published in the early 1980s.

The Threepenny Doctor: Doctor Jelley of Hackney by "A People's Autobiography of Hackney", ten short anecdotes from elderly Hackney residents paint a picture of this eccentric local figure who, before the NHS, had been more likely to prescribe a hearty steak to his patients than medicine they couldn't afford. Published by Centerprise in 1974.

kept cropping up in interviews. And we were really struck when we came to realise that he had performed abortions, how tolerantly that was referred to. He used to help women when they were "in trouble". And, during the First World War, a husband comes back and the wife's been pregnant and had an abortion and he gets to hear, and he shops Dr Jelley who then does a prison term. And nobody spoke with anything but sympathy for Dr Jelley as far as I remember. So we just took snippets out of different tapes and made a collage of them.

Next came *Rebels With A Cause* (1975) by Barry Burke, a history of Hackney Trades Council, *Working Lives: Volume One* and *Working Lives: Volume Two* (1976 and 1977) a two volume collection of accounts of working lives from 1905–1945 and 1945–1977 respectively, and *The Island: The life and death of an East London community 1870–1970* (1979), an oral history of a remarkably tight and somewhat isolated community, contained within a few streets in Hackney Downs. "A People's Autobiography of Hackney" group member, Neil Martinson, who had first got involved in Centerprise as a school student, was hired by the publishing project in 1976, at first working alongside his former teacher Ken Worpole. He remembers the "extraordinarily ambitious" *Working Lives: Volume Two*, which contained thirteen accounts of working life in Hackney, either transcribed from interviews or written by the workers themselves. It was hoped the book gave "a sense of the usefulness of the work people do and its service to others".[149] The accounts of working life included that of a hairdresser, mortuary technician, health visitor, machinist and teacher amongst others. A photographer documented each person's working life in detail, taking up to five hundred photographs, from which twenty or thirty were chosen to accompany the text. Neil co-ordinated the photographs, book design and production, working alongside group convenor Richard Gray who brought together "A People's Autobiography of Hackney's" work on the text.

[149] *Working Lives*, 1977, 6.

Neil recalls:

We did 5,000 copies of the first print run, because that was the only way we could keep the unit price down. And I think, there's 110 pictures in it by five photographers. Nobody got paid, and I'm pretty sure [the photographers] paid for our own materials as well. So it was an extraordinary undertaking, to actually do it, and it cost quite a lot of money to produce. I think it's really good, it stands the test of time.

The process was not without its hiccups, as Neil describes:

There was a moment when we got the book back when I had a heart attack pretty much, because, one of the accounts is by a mortuary technician, and we had an agreement to take the pictures of him at work on the basis that you couldn't see the faces of dead people. And we had cropped the pictures, and the way you would crop them then was you'd put tracing paper on the print and you would mark it up. Anyway, the 5,000 copies came back, and we were going through it, and there was this face staring at us from the slab. We thought, shit. So we desperately looked to find the mark-up we did, and the mark-up was accurate; the printers had made a mistake. It would have been disastrous, because we couldn't possibly afford to reprint it. So what they did is, they cut out the page by hand and inserted reprints, 5,000 of them, which was very, very fortunate.

A writers' group run by black arts worker Dorothea Smartt (second from left), early 1990s. Copyright © Sherlee Mitchell.

Publishing longer and more complex books came at a cost. Sue Shrapnel remembered that the making of *Working Lives Volume Two* made the wider collective sit up and take notice of what the publishing project was up to: "by the time you'd had all that, there was a 'never again' feeling, and a feeling that we must assert control over what the publishing project does. It can't just talk us into investments of this size. I mean it was a huge investment, the figures going through the books traumatised some people; the parcels of books arriving traumatised everybody else. There was just so much of it. You clearly were going into a different league, and everyone thought, uh-uh."[150]

Publishing workers brought each book they wanted to publish to the

150 Shrapnel, Interview with Sue Shrapnel (later Gardener) by Maggie Hewitt.

The Lime Green Mystery

A contact sheet showing photographs of Lotte Moos taken by Maggie Hewitt for the cover of her publication with Centerprise. The image chosen can be seen above right and below is the book cover, *Time to be Bold* by Lotte Moos (1981). Photographs courtesy of Maggie Hewitt.

Buildings have history

I took the photo on her first volume of poetry, *Time to Be Bold*. We didn't have photographers to do that, if you were in commercial publishing you would. She lived really near Victoria Park, so we went round with the camera taking photos in front of all the trees. We had just got back, and there were a couple at the end, and she said, "I'll take one of you". And then when we got in, I realised there was one more shot on, and I just clicked it, and that's the one on the cover.
— Maggie Hewitt

Centerprise collective for approval before proceeding. There was plenty of choice when it came to deciding what to publish, in 1986, for instance, Centerprise received around seventy unsolicited manuscripts.[151] Their selection was made based on what had been chosen before to avoid repetition, with priority given to previously unpublished, local authors. Authors who did not live in Hackney were referred on to their local publishing project, if one existed. Each book signified not only an investment of money, but a political decision about what and who should be represented.

Seeking to further democratise the writing and publishing process, Centerprise began to organise the Hackney Writers Workshop in 1976, one of the first and most long-running of many writing groups that Centerprise would host over the years. Such writing groups were, as Dorothea Smartt, black arts worker from 1990 to 1993 explains, places "of beginnings … where people could bring their tender new selves, new to writing, and find a kind of supportive and encouraging space."

The Hackney Writers Workshop published several volumes of collected poetry and prose, alongside individual works by group members such as Savitri Hensman, who wrote her fiercely anti-racist poetry collection *Flood at the Door* (1979), while still at school. Fellow poet, Lotte Moos's volume of poems, *Time to be Bold*, (1981) was considered so important it was printed with money fronted by other group members as Centerprise was in the midst of a financial crisis at the time. In her introduction to *Time to be Bold* Lotte describes her journey as a writer. As a child growing up in Berlin, amidst the German Jewish intelligentsia, she had made up stories but then "real life" in the thirties "put the boot in" until, having escaped to London with her husband and fellow poet, Siege, "the blacked out rooms and the horrors of World War II finally boxed me in, making me fall back on something I had almost forgotten". She wrote, but had no feedback, and next came "flapping past, the years of nappy-washing, pram-pushing and general child-adoration". Since joining the Hackney Writers Workshop, she wrote, "the sluice gates seem to have opened". She explained:

> **How does the Hackney Writers Workshop work? Assembled in a small room up two flights of stairs, some – coming straight from a late shift; some – housewives; some schoolgirls (at one time, ages ranged from sixteen to seventy), we fumble with our bits of paper and, after some hesitation, admit – yes, we have something to read. These are the people for whom we write or, rather, without whom we mightn't write, or not enough.**[152]

Roger Mills, a young writer from Hackney, published a book of prose with Centerprise, *A Comprehensive Education* (1979), about his time at school and the ways in which he felt his education had let him down. He describes the group process as "like a tennis game where ideas would come backwards and forwards". It was this process that inspired him to publish:

> **"I didn't really have an idea of writing a book. I thought, I've got**

[151] Centerprise Trust Ltd, 'Centerprise Annual Report 1986.'

[152] Lotte Moos, *Time to Be Bold* (London: Centerprise Trust Ltd., 1981), 5–7.

Maggie Hewitt (left), Sue May (centre) and Sue Shrapnel (right), members of the Hackney Writers' Workshop rehearsing before a reading, 1980s. Photograph courtesy of Maggie Hewitt.

nothing to write about except myself. So I'd take autobiographical little pieces along to the Writers' Workshop every week, and people there suggested, 'Why don't you stick 'em all together and make a book out of it?' So that did come out of the workshopping process. And people would comment about what I had written, or, ask about certain aspects of this or that, why didn't I write about that?"

As Lotte carefully noted, the role of convenor within the writers' workshop remained crucial: "the transition from spontaneity to a more critical approach calls for much tact from the 'convenor'."[153] This was a paid position, most often taken by a member of Centerprise staff.

Publishing workers past and present, along with other Centerprise workers like Sue Shrapnel, tended to join the writing workshops, thereby experiencing something of what it was like to be on the other side of the editor-writer dynamic. Maggie Hewitt remembers that although she was used to speaking publicly as a former teacher, sharing her writing with the group was different: "People brought work to the group, and, everybody tried to be both supportive and critical, and that can be quite hard. And in a way that's why there needed to be a sort of equality where everybody was exposing themselves. I mean you're very exposed when you're reading something you've written, especially if it's very personal. I mean it does vary, some

[153] Ibid., 8.

people were maybe more political, slightly more distanced in the way they wrote really. But, it's still quite a brave thing to do, to take that risk."

The publishing project and writers' workshops developed alongside similar initiatives elsewhere. Hackney Writers' Workshop was inspired by the Basement Writers group in Stepney, founded by Chris Searle, of the 'Stepney School Strike.' In 1976 the inaugural meeting of the Federation of Worker Writers and Community Publishers (FWWCP) was held at Centerprise, with eight writing and publishing groups from across the UK in attendance. "The Fed" as it became known, quickly spread across the country and supported the growth of worker-writing. Ideas and methods were shared from one group to another and some new projects, such as The People's Press in Milton Keynes, were established as a direct result of seeing the publishing project at Centerprise.[154] Other bookshop and publishing projects in London were often closely connected. People involved in Centerprise went on to similar projects elsewhere, for instance Roger Mills worked at the similar Tower Hamlets Arts Project and convenor of "A People's Autobiography of Hackney", Richard Gray, went on to be a publishing worker at The Bookplace, Peckham's community bookshop. By 1983 when young writer Nick Pollard moved to Hackney from Sheffield he was able to seamlessly leave his local writing group, Heely Writers, and join Hackney Writers' Workshop for the short period he lived in London, contributing his writing to group publications like *Where There's Smoke* (1984). These publications were distributed to other community bookshops across the country, as Nick remembers: "So, when I came back to Sheffield I could see copies of *Where There's Smoke* in the local left-wing bookshop. So it felt like a real book, because it was actually being sold in a bookshop."

The publications produced reflected the changing preoccupations of the times. From the 1980s onwards Centerprise published a greater number of works by women and people from ethnic minorities, and where possible both, such as *Breaking the Silence* (1984), a collection of writing by Asian women, Pauline Wiltshire's autobiography, *Living and Winning* (1985), which detailed her life and struggles as a disabled, black woman in London and Jamaica and the collection of poetry and prose *Not All Roses* (1987) by the Black Anthology Group. New collective writing groups provided spaces for women, young people and black people to work together on their writing: Hackney Women Writers, the all-women Day Writers and Night Writers, Young Centerprise Writers and black writers' groups such as the Words, Sounds and Power Writers' Workshop.

"A People's Autobiography of Hackney" had ended in 1981 but new avenues to explore local history were found. At a meeting of the Federation of Worker Writers and Community Publishers, Maggie found out about the "singing strikers"; young women who in the 1920s had worked in the Rego and Poliakoff clothing factories and had struck in protest when their jobs were moving out of Hackney. To raise money and morale they had roamed the streets singing songs about their strike set to popular tunes of the day.[155]

[154] Roger Kitchen, 'Dig Where You Stand: Using Local Lives to Generate Community in Milton Keynes', *Oral History* 40, no. 2 (Autumn 2012): 93–98.

[155] Harris, 'The Federation of Worker Writers and Community Publishers – Gemeinde Arbeit Und Identitätsbildung'.

Their songs were published by the Communist Party, which is how the memory of the strike was preserved. Centerprise republished the booklet of strike songs and a research group was formed to interview workers about the rag trade. An exhibition was produced about the strike, which drew attention to the problems Hackney's garment workers continued to face in the 1980s. Maggie remembers how researching the songs gave the group a valuable insight into the different people involved in the strike: "The strikers were nearly all women, and some of them were very young, they could have been fourteen, and had no experience of doing anything political before. And we got in touch with Sandra Kerr, a very political folk singer, and she said she would join us and research the songs. So she simply asked her mother, who remembered the songs of the thirties, and came back with tunes to a lot of them. And what was really interesting, she could tell from the language that some were definitely written by the men, because they were full of solidarity forever. And the ones that were written by the women, the language was completely different, and that was really fascinating, to discover that by singing them."

The work of the publishing project ranged "from the very routine to the very stimulating", as Maggie wrote in her report to the collective after three months in the post, "a lot of it is moving boxes around, addressing envelopes and sending off orders."[156] Neil Martinson describes the job of publishing worker as "effectively running a small business", having had to work out himself the cheapest way to source paper and warehouse it, for instance. Bernadette Halpin, publishing project worker from 1990 to 1993 depicts the work as demanding: "publishing a book is a very, very time-consuming process. You're doing all of it. You're talking to the author, you're getting the manuscript ready. That is a full-time job in itself, but on top of that, you were expected to have workshops and book launches. And running a writing workshop is hard work."

First, as Bernadette describes, there was the work of supporting individual writers. This did not always lead to a publication; some writers were helped to complete writing simply so they could share it with friends and family. Once a decision had been made to publish an author's work, a publishing worker might work closely with them for six months, a year, or even more to prepare their manuscript. Some authors would have their words taped and transcribed if they were unable to write themselves, while the majority would bring in their own manuscripts which the publishing worker would edit. The role of editor demanded a great deal of tact and sensitivity, as Bernadette explains:

> It's in a way the most sensitive thing in the world, isn't it, to sit with someone and talk to them about what they've written? About a poem that isn't quite working, maybe, and they know it's not quite working, and you're trying to work out why not. It demands an ear for language, sophistication about language, to be able to read something and understand why it isn't working. To understand the

[156] Hewitt, 'Maggie's Three Month Review'.

writer. Because if you're saying to someone, "I don't think this poem quite works," you know, it's quite a tough thing to say to somebody. This is their baby, this is their short story, this is their novel. Some of them used to bring their work in to me and say, "I've spent eight and a half years writing this novel." And I'd think, "Oh Christ – it's going to take me eight and half years to read it!" It draws upon a lot of different kinds of personal and professional skills. And, a real love for the person you're working with – I mean that in a generalised, universal sense.

Writers would not have found this kind of dedicated input to improve their work with commercial publishers, as many of the publishing workers point out. For instance, the book Bernadette was most proud of, *The 43 Group* (1993) by Morris Beckman, was initially, she says, a very "chaotic" manuscript. Morris was Jewish, had grown up in Hackney, and had served with the merchant navy on the Arctic convoys of World War II. Coming back from the war, he and other Jewish ex-servicemen and women were disgusted to find British fascists holding meetings around Hackney, often in Ridley Road Market. They decided to set up a group to fight back against the fascists by physically closing down their meetings. There were forty-three at their first meeting and so they became The 43 Group. Bernadette worked with him for over six months reordering and editing the manuscript until they were ready

Author Betty Voden carrying a decorated cake at the launch party of her book *One Over the Baker's Dozen*, 1985. Photograph courtesy of Maggie Hewitt.

for publication. When complete, Bernadette was "humbled" by the book's launch party: "It happened at a big hall or auditorium in Golders Green. And the book had just arrived from the printers. I literally drove up there with cartons of this book. It was attended by thousands of Jewish people, older Jewish people. I can't tell you how important that book was, because it was a book about resistance."

The publishing project aimed to encourage writers to make their work public in many ways; sharing writing with others in the workshops and reading their work at live events as well as putting their words into print. Once complete, books were launched with parties, often held at Centerprise in the coffee bar with accompanying exhibitions showing how the book was produced. The events were open to all, as Pauline Brown remembers: "the atmosphere in these launching party was quite happy … It was very enjoyable. The words in the book, makes your spirit be lifted up, makes you feel energised. It makes you feel really relaxed in ourselves, we enjoy ourselves. We had a lot to eat, and drink, and we had fun." Cakes, themed with the book would be made, and food laid out. Authors would read from their books as Jean Milloy remembers: "people were just so proud with what they had achieved. So they were often quite moving events."

Events held at Centerprise had a unique atmosphere because of the incredibly diverse mixture of people that often gathered together under one roof. One especially memorable night was a reading held by "acclaimed African-American" poet Essex Hemphil on 11 March 1992.[157] An unusually large audience of over fifty people gathered to hear Essex read his poems, as black arts worker Dorothea Smartt (DS) and publishing worker Bernadette Halpin (BH) describe:

DS:
> And I remember hosting Essex Hemphil, who was a really amazing, African American poet, writer, activist. So here was this very out black gay man, with his very explicit poetry.

BH:
> I remember. Yes.

DS:
> It was quite a coup to have him read at Centerprise.

BH:
> It rushes back. I remember the explicit poetry. When you used that word, I remembered.

DS:
> And I mean, his work was very out there.

BH:
> The women from the kitchen were there. When the word cock came up, don't you remember?

DS:
> Yeah. Yeah.

[157] Centerprise Trust Ltd, 'London Arts Board: Quarterly Activity Details Report. January – March 1992', 1992, A Hackney Autobiography, Bishopsgate Institute.

BH:
> And it came up quite often …

DS:
> It came up quite a lot in his work. So there were the people who always came to Centerprise events, including the kind of, mature black women who were …

BH:
> Church-going West Indian ladies.

DS:
> Yeah, who ran the café. And, a whole bunch of black gay men and black lesbians and anybody else who had heard of Essex and was there. And so it was a very popular evening, it was full. And he didn't censor it or anything for the community. And what was great about the reading, it was predominantly black that evening, and there was this age range of various people. At the end of the evening, I went and [talked to one of the coffee bar workers]. And said, "Oh, how did you feel?" She said, "Him have a very nice reading voice," was what she said. "Him have a very nice reading voice." And I remember Essex really, really, you know, enjoying that night. And, it brought together all these different kind of people, who wouldn't necessarily have all been in the room together at the same thing.

From 1991, Bernadette and Dorothea organised a monthly night for women in the coffee bar, the Word Up Women's Café, with every third café for black women only. The nights were open-mic and offered a vast diversity of women performers: Egyptian dancers, stand-up comics, singers, poets and other writers of all kinds. Bernadette would be the MC and "thought it was really important to look the part. So I would go home, put on a tuxedo jacket." Dorothea remembers her as "always very dashing on the night." Bernadette says "the queue would be around the block" and they would get really crowded on special evenings, like for International Women's Day but "nobody complained. They were good nights." In 1993, a collection of lesbian poetry, *Words from the Women's Café* was published, compiling some of the performers' writing.

Bernadette and Dorothea were the last publishing workers to use the small room at the top of the building as the publishing project ended in 1993, and was replaced by a literature development project. This was one of the first of a new kind of writing development project, which Dorothea describes as "the other side of the work that we did, working with writers, running writing groups, giving people advice and information about publishing." Eva Lewin, who worked at the project from 1994 to 2006 explains that community publishing projects were no longer viable in the mid-1990s because: "the amount it cost to produce a book, and then to sell it, meant that the public funding really wasn't going very far. So they [the funders] wanted an initiative that might support a bigger range of writers, and work in a variety of ways

The Word Up Women's Café, early 1990s. Copyright © Sherlee Mitchell.

with writers. And they particularly wanted to support black and Asian writers." Unlike the publishing project, it did not bring out new books, although it did publish writers' work in a magazine, *Calabash*, started by another worker, Kadija George, and aimed at writers of African and Asian descent. Bernadette and Dorothea regretted the loss of the publishing project, as although time-consuming they saw publishing as the "logical conclusion" of working with writers. They worried about training writers up, only to leave them "to flounder in a commercial world that doesn't necessarily want to publish them."

The launch party at Centerprise for *Taken for a Ride* by Ruth Parsons, an account of working on the buses, 1980. Photograph courtesy of Maggie Hewitt.

4: An attempted jail break

When the bookshop first opened, Margaret Gosley remembers Glenn Thompson encountering an initial reluctance at the Penguin publishing house when they were asked to support the new venture.[158] The publishing house was worried, she says, that as "the working classes don't read; how was a bookshop [in Hackney] going to succeed?" That the bookshop quickly had some commercial success proved, Centerprise argued, that there was a hunger for literature in working class areas like Hackney. Centerprise's assertion that a bookshop and local publishing project were "cultural rights" for local, working class people was just one expression of a wider challenge to dominant ideas that determined, not only who could create and enjoy culture, but what counted as culture.[159] The academic discipline of Cultural Studies was just beginning to study working class cultural practices, the growing Community Arts movement hoped to establish "ordinary" and "working class" experience as a subject for art,[160] while the History Workshop movement experimented with methodologies, like oral history, that could help make the recording of history a democratic pursuit. The do-it-yourself ethos of this cultural movement, combined with relatively recent technological developments like tape recorders, offset-litho printing and rub-down typefaces like Letraset made participating easier than ever before.

[158] Penguin did later offer significant assistance to Centerprise, donating them shelving for their shops and extending them credit.

[159] Worpole, *Local Publishing & Local Culture*, 2.

[160] S. Wetherell, 'Painting the Crisis: Community Arts and the Search for the "Ordinary" in 1970s and '80s London', *History Workshop Journal* 76, no. 1 (1 October 2013): 235–49, doi:10.1093/hwj/dbt008.

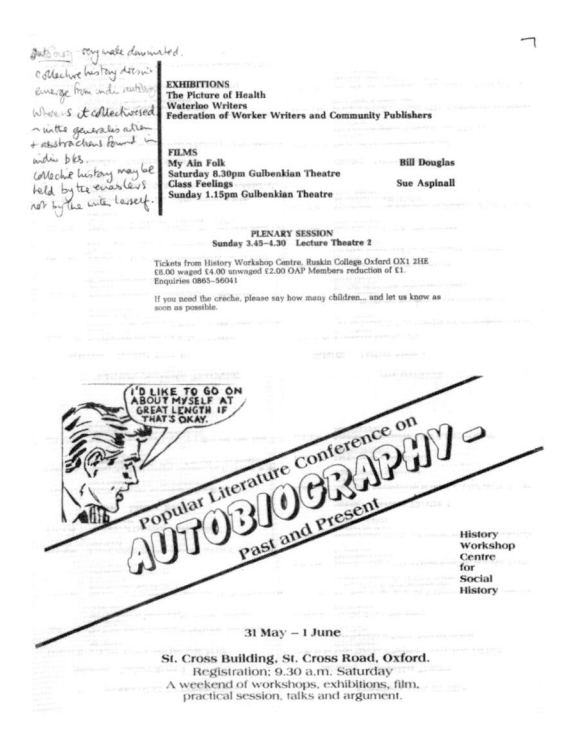

Programme for a History Workshop Conference on Autobiography, held in 1986. Photograph courtesy of Maggie Hewitt.

By publishing local authors Centerprise sought to give voice to people whose experiences were largely unrepresented within mainstream culture at the time and it was hoped that readers of books by local authors would find recognisable representations of their own experiences and interests, and thereby feel enabled to write and publish themselves. "A People's Autobiography of Hackney's" work recording local history was also, as Neil Martinson describes, "about validation of the lives that you lead." They published autobiographies of local people because that form of writing was especially able to "express the feelings of both writer and reader", Ken Worpole wrote.[161] As Stuart Hood put it: "Autobiography is an attempted jail-break. The reader tunnels through the same dark."[162] The project chose the autobiographies that they published carefully, seeking those that were best able to "clarify, express with precision, stand for and carry the weight of the typical and common experiences of a much larger group of people who could find and recognise large parts of their own lives within a particular autobiography."[163]

Readers' actual responses to the books published were, however, subjective and hard to evaluate. As publishing worker Maggie Hewitt describes "The thing about books is, you work very hard on a publication and then, somehow, it disappears, it flies off. And unless someone gets back to you, you don't actually know where it goes to or what the impact is." For some the impact was known to be dramatic. Roger Mills, then a recent school-leaver, describes discovering books by Vivian Usherwood and Ron Barnes at Centerprise as the moment he realised he too could become a writer: "I can honestly say, they're two of the most important books I've ever read, not because they were two of the best books I've ever read, but, the fact that they existed. I thought, 'blimey, there's a black kid and a middle-aged taxi driver, and they've both written books.' This was a revelation to me, that such people were *allowed* to write books, let alone have them published." Some others were clearly unmoved by the publishing project's commitment to shining a light on "typical and common" experiences. In his afterword to his second book Ron Barnes wrote "After my first book was published, a number of people told me about other people they knew who had had bad experiences in their childhood. Whist relating these experiences to me they have more or less suggested that I was not the only one to experience distress in childhood, so why was it necessary to write what I did?"[164]

At least Ron Barnes' writing had got people talking, even if not everyone liked it. Another problem, described by writer Eveline Marius in 1984, was that she felt her own African-Caribbean community was unimpressed by her writing: "The ordinary people in the community, right, members of the ethnic community, alright you write, but they don't really look upon it as a great achievement because they don't really understand the essence of your writing and what you are saying in your poetry. You have to explain line for line what you mean. But when you look at the middle class people and the educated people, they get more of an insight into what you write than the ordinary people in your community."[165]

[161] Worpole, Local Publishing & Local Culture, 6.

[162] Stuart Hood, *Pebbles from My Skull* in ibid.

[163] Ibid.

[164] Ron Barnes, *Coronation Cups and Jam Jars: A Portrait of an East End Family through Three Generations* (London: Centerprise, 1976), 204.

[165] Eveline Marius, Interview with Eveline Marius by Maggie Hewitt, 13 September 1984, A Hackney Autobiography, Bishopsgate Institute.

The processes by which the books were produced were constantly evolving in search of a more democratic way of working, and yet differences between writers and readers, group members and group convenors, teachers and students, writers and editors, interviewers and interviewees, remained. As the 1970s gave way to the 1980s, ethnic and gendered identities increasingly overtook class in debates about the use of language in Centerprise's books and how the project worked with writers.

We not I

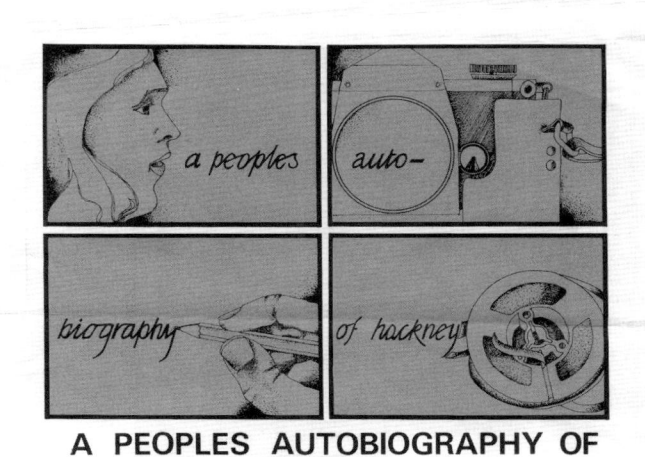

The first poster for "A People's Autobiography of Hackney", 1970s. Courtesy of Ken Worpole.

Ken Worpole wrote in 1977 that the publishing project's early "editorial policy … was [still] very much a matter of individual judgement within certain guide-lines; politically different, economically different, but not structurally different really from the ways in which commercial publishers make choices."[166] It was by working in groups, such as "A People's Autobiography of Hackney" and Hackney Writers' Workshop, that Centerprise hoped to forge a new, more democratic kind of editorial relationship with writers.

"A People's Autobiography of Hackney" gathered together local history enthusiasts, radical historians drawn from the History Workshop milieu and local sixth form students. Members included Israel Renson, a local pharmacist, Albert Cullington, a retired clerk and former mayor of Hackney, Ronnie Barden, a local businessman and later Conservative leader of Redbridge Council, Anna Davin, a historian and feminist and younger people, including Roger Mills and Neil Martinson. Their ages ranged from sixteen to seventy-five. The group met regularly to discuss the oral histories they had recorded and decide together who they should interview next and what to produce from the material collected. Neil says it was a "very democratic process". The meetings blurred the lines between contributor and collector as Anna Davin describes: "I know that sometimes somebody had done a tape and would play it, and then we'd all discuss it. And basically, the older members of the group would then become the experts and we would ask them about, 'What did that mean?' or, 'Do you remember that too?' or, 'Where was that?' from the tape that we listened to. And sometimes the person interviewed would be there as well. I think sometimes it was more thematic, we might be trying to explore work or some theme, and pulling things together both from the memories of people there and from whatever interviewing had been happening."

Attempts were made to give interviewees control of their texts, whether or not they joined the group. For instance, one of the earliest autobiographies published, Arthur Newton's *Years of Change: Autobiography of a Hackney Shoemaker* (1974), was produced after the original interview was transcribed and given back to Mr Newton. He then delivered them a manuscript in perfect copperplate handwriting, without a trace of the orality of the original source, peppered with his own reflections.[167] Others, like Emily Bishop, a former seamstress who contributed to the first volume of *Working Lives*, insisted on writing their own accounts, and in doing so deployed literary techniques to tell their stories in a way they could not have done verbally. Emily Bishop's writing begins by describing a scene from the outside: "Pre-1914 in the East End of London – drab to say the least. Two figures walking in the early morning streets."[168] The figures are revealed to be the author and her mother, and Emily Bishop then switches into the first person to give an account of her working life as an embroiderer.

The attitudes of the people involved were a crucial part of this attempt to distribute editorial authority more widely. Richard Gray, who took over as group convenor from Ken Worpole, said he tried

all the time to keep it in your mind that, this is about doing it together. This is we, not I. So, that was always at the forefront of my mind, in doing the, quote unquote, "editorial work" on *Working Lives*. And bringing stuff to the group. Because we met fortnightly, so I would

---

[166] Worpole, *Local Publishing & Local Culture*.

[167] Ibid.

[168] *Working Lives: A People's Autobiography of Hackney*. (London; London: Hackney WEA; Centerprise Pub. Project, 1976), 9.

basically be bringing my work to the next meeting for people to read and give their feedback on, and then what was decided in that fortnight's meeting made my work for the next fortnight.

Gradually the group began to move away from individual autobiographies and take on broader histories, as Richard describes:

> The conversations would move on to, well, we were a group, why didn't we look at group experience? We were doing individual books, but actually if we called ourselves community historians, working class historians, we were looking for the collective, for the cooperative, for the people working together, so why didn't we do a group autobiography? Not instead of but as well as, we weren't going to stop doing individual books. So, that's how that idea of doing something more group-orientated, more collaborative, came into being.

Ken Worpole, writing after the first five years of the publishing project, described how the *Working Lives* project saw an increase in group members taking on servicing functions, like interviewing and transcribing; "very importantly, group editing has begun to replace individual editing".[169]

Group members were involved for different reasons. Some were motivated primarily by a passion for local history while others hoped the project would be a vehicle for social change. Ken Jacobs, a postman and photographer joined "A People's Autobiography of Hackney" because of his interest in local history. In an interview with Julia and Richard Gray (RG), Ken Jacobs (KJ) describes his political background as:

> Labour, we were brought up as staunch Labour people. I was a member of the Young Socialists in Hackney for a couple of years, when they were based in Graham Road. I've still got my Young Socialists badge. ... We used to go and heckle Oswald Mosley when he spoke at Ridley Road.

However, he distances himself from his fairly radical youth, saying: "I was never really that into politics. I think, I only went there because there was nice girls in [the group]."

When it came to Centerprise, he said just the label "community centre" gave it away as a left-wing project. This, he says, could have put him off entirely but instead it wasn't an issue as:

> I was there for one reason, and that was to do this history project, be it talking to old people about their past, or the Island project, or the *Working Lives* projects, that was all I was interested in and what I enjoyed doing. And everybody there was friendly enough. It was not as if, you know, people were at each other's throats all the time and back-biting, to me, it didn't come into it at all.

[169] Worpole, *Local Publishing & Local Culture*, 11.

He felt that, in comparison with himself, most of the people involved were an "educated load of left-wingers":

KJ:

Oh, one of the things that came over to me was that, most of the people there were quite educated compared to me. I just had the basic state education. I wasn't very articulate with the way I spoke. I still ain't. You know, not … And to me, kind of, it was an educated load of left-wingers, and, I was involved with them in this, through this, the Centerprise project.

RG:

Mm. But you kept coming.

KJ:

I kept coming, because I enjoyed it. I enjoyed the company as well. Made some good friends.

RG:

Right. Right. And you did actually … You're being very modest. As time went on, you got involved, especially with the Island, you became one of the people who did what those educated left-wingers had done in the beginning, people like me, we were the ones who had done the interviews, and done the transcribing. And you gradually got more involved, because, you said you went to do one of the interviews for *Working Lives: Volume One*.

KJ:

Mhm, which I also transcribed as well.

RG:

And you transcribed it as well. So, hang on a minute. You are starting to do … What's interesting from the historical point of view is, we've got the picture of Centerprise being started up by a group of well-educated lefties, if you like, and them wanting to start doing community work and with this project, "A People's Autobiography", starting to do community history, or people's history, and then the interesting thing is that as the group goes on, over the years, the lines begin to get a bit blurred. So you, as somebody born and bred in Hackney, comes along, gets involved, then starts going out and doing interviews, as well as being one of the people being interviewed, or one of the people doing the writing. So you go along and you take part in that interview for *Working Lives: Volume One*, and then, you come up, the pub conversation with Roger. You gradually get drawn in, and we're planning a new project there, we're planning what we're going to do next when we finish doing *Working Lives*. So gradually you're getting drawn in to running the group as well as –

KJ:

Well I wouldn't say running a group, but …

RG:
> Oh okay, well, it's interesting to hear what you thought of it all.

KJ:
> I had, I suppose you could say that, because of my connections with the Island, and Roger, Roger Mills's connection with the Island as well, that, we were the instigators of it all, obviously, and we, we were looked upon as, I think, as the leaders of it.

Here, Richard Gray's perception of how the group worked is not quite the same as Ken Jacobs', who felt the need to interject to qualify "I wouldn't say running a group" when Richard describes the process by which Ken had gradually become more involved. However, Ken Jacobs did tentatively describe himself as an "instigator" and "leader" of the Island project, which he and Roger Mills had first thought up over a pint in the pub. One of the things Ken Jacobs did for the Island project was produce a tape slide projection using his photographs and the oral histories, which he presented at a History Workshop conference, thereby performing an explicitly intellectual function within the group.

The politics of some group members meant, as Richard Gray says, they were on the "look-out" for certain things: "examples of, working class solidarity, resistance, and a certain socialist or certainly Labour voting tradition." These assumptions, which threatened that what was looked for would be what was found,[170] were at least somewhat challenged by the process of interviewing people. As Richard Gray explains: "you become aware that actually the politics of the people that you're talking to about their work are very different." Similarly, Ken Worpole describes how his perception of working class family life changed during the process of interviewing people: "The things that did really surprise me was the degree to which a lot of people we interviewed had actually been brought up either by grandparents or aunts and uncles, and not by their own direct parents, either because there was too much poverty, or the house was too small, there were too many brothers and sisters, siblings, and they began to get farmed out to relatives who didn't have children, or because they actually couldn't get on with their parents, and would go and live with an uncle, or an aunt. It had never occurred to me that that the working class tight family group was actually much more negotiable." Learning therefore cut both ways, which was part of the point.

The group worked well for almost a decade, partly because compromises were made by its members, who all had slightly different motivations to be involved. In an interview recorded in 1984 Neil Martinson explained he would have liked the group to have taken a more explicitly radical approach to the study of the past, but had realized with hindsight that to do so would have risked losing those members who did not share his enthusiasm.[171] The focus on collective process in groups such as "A People's Autobiography of Hackney" was pre-figurative, in that it attempted to show through its practice what a more equal society might be like. Richard Gray says that

---

[170] This is paraphrasing poet Howard Mingham's poem 'To scholars and Ken Worpole', published in *Waters of the Night* (2013). Howard Mingham was a member of Hackney Writers' Workshop in the late 1970s and early 1980s.

[171] Martinson, Interview with Neil Martinson by Maggie Hewitt.

for him "there was a kind of a glow of going there on a Wednesday evening, because the rest of my working life I found very hard in Hackney … I did not enjoy my day job. So it was that sense of relief and actually, alright, the world isn't the way it should be, but, there is a group of us here who can make it the way it should be for an evening, for this two hours, and when we go for a drink afterwards, and maybe when we come out with the next book, we'll actually help change the world towards what it ought to be."

Just writing it down

By interviewing people and producing books from their words, Centerprise transformed spoken language into text, raising the problem of what should be done about the author or narrator's dialect. Poetry and prose were sometimes written in dialect, especially by young black authors influenced by reggae and dub, but autobiographies tended to be written in standard English, a decision that Centerprise workers, who wanted the publications to promote the parity of different forms of language, grudgingly accepted. Richard Gray describes using interviews in books as a negotiation with the interviewee:

> I would say the majority of people wanted their statement to be done according to the rules of standard written English, and if they had the skills they would check it themselves, and say, "I don't want to say that, that doesn't look good on paper." … They didn't want to look stupid basically, that's how they felt. Because standard English has that aura about it. So even though I might have said, "Well this would sound really good, if we publish it the way you spoke it," I didn't often get away with that.

It was in the publications produced by the Hackney Reading Centre that the question of whether or not to publish in dialect really came to the fore. Many of the students were migrants, the majority from the Caribbean, and therefore spoke various forms of Caribbean English. In the 1970s, as the group enrolling in literacy classes nationwide begun to include more people from Commonwealth countries, Sue Shrapnel reflected that this "shifted the emphasis from the class nature to the post-colonial nature of the literacy problem."[172] Writing about the reading centre's writing and publishing work with African-Caribbean students, Jud Stone and Irene Schwab wrote that "the issue of language constantly arose" in their work.[173]

The reading centre's approach to language had been formed partly through exposure to the ideas of educational theorists like Basil Bernstein, as Jud explains: "It's the people in power who decide what's the right kind of language, and what's standard, and what's good, and what's bad. And so we were interrogating that and saying, 'No, that's not right.' I mean, we had a phrase 'a language is a dialect with an army'. And we were looking at the history of the English language, which is a mongrel language if there ever

[172] Shrapnel, Interview with Sue Shrapnel (later Gardener) by Maggie Hewitt.

[173] Schwab and Stone, *Language, Writing and Publishing: Work with Afro-Caribbean Students.*

was one, with all the different influences that have come in. And languages change over time and you can't control it." Irene Schwab mentions the importance of discussing these ideas about language with students: "A lot of students who … had been educated in the Caribbean, had been told that their Creole language wasn't correct English; they'd been told it was broken English, and it was bad English. … We were trying to talk to them about varieties of English not being bad or broken, but just different, and that it's okay to write in the language you speak, whether that's Creole or whether it's cockney London, or whatever. So that was a big thing for us, and that was why we published books that were written as people speak".

The "language experience approach" to teaching literacy, where the students' own words are used to teach them to read, depends on the phrases spoken by the student being transcribed by the tutor exactly as they are said, as otherwise the student will not be able to use their memory to help them decode the writing. This can be difficult, as Sue Shrapnel recognised:

> I think it's a skill you have to cultivate, to retain the exact words anybody uses, to the point where you can write them down. Because people don't speak at dictation speed when they're doing language experience with you. And, you get better at saying, "Hold on, hold on," but you may still have twenty or thirty words to get down. And you have to learn, whoever you're with, you have to increase your ability to retain that word-for-word until you've got it down. And if you're not very good at the particular English that they're speaking, you'll almost certainly rephrase it as you put it down.
>
> I think I'm better at it now than I was, because I'm better acquainted with the grammars of Caribbean English for example. So I don't standardise. I mean, when I wasn't that familiar, the only way I could retain the stuff was by standardising it, by effectively doing a mental translation and standardising some of the features that I didn't know the pattern of within their own right. So while we said we were trying to write it down word-for-word, I think, for years we weren't.[174]

How students felt about the language experience approach varied greatly. Sue remembered one student who was frustrated about being asked to speak about her own experiences saying: "Well, you keep asking me to say this stuff about back home. That was all right for him [her tutor] because he didn't know that, but I knew that. I wanted to do something I didn't know." Another student "nailed her colours to the mast" by writing a piece that said "I'm not going to change my accent for nobody. If someone don't understand me, that's their lookout."[175]

Isaac Gordon studied at the reading centre for ten years and, unusually, published two books about his life through Centerprise, *Going Where the Work Is* (1979) and *It Can Happen* (1985). Perhaps because his writing was sustained over several years, it is an interesting case study of how issues of

[174] Shrapnel, Interview with Sue Shrapnel (later Gardener) by Maggie Hewitt.

[175] Ibid.

Above left: **Isaac Gordon, reading centre student, standing against the wall at a book launch party at Centerprise, 1983. Photograph courtesy of Maggie Hewitt.**
Above right: **book jacket of** *Going Where the Work Is* **by Isaac Gordon, 1979. Cover photograph copyright © Neil Martinson.**

language and power played out during the making of his books. Isaac Gordon could read very little when he first came to the reading centre. His first book, *Going Where the Work Is*, developed out of various learning exercises and was dictated to his tutor, Jud Stone. The book's afterword says:

> This is work we do over one year and six months.
> We start off
> and it growing more and more.
> Then it getting interesting.
> So we decide to put it together.
> I am telling Jud about my life
> and she just write it down.
> I like to do it
> and I hope other people like to read it.
>
> Isaac & Jud
> March 1978 [176]

[176] Isaac Gordon, *Going Where the Work Is* (London: Hackney Reading Centre, 1979), 34.

What Isaac and Jud did together to prepare the book was, of course, more complicated than just writing down Isaac's words. A detailed account of the process of publishing Isaac's books is contained in *Language, Writing and Publishing*, Irene Schwab and Jud Stone's account of the reading centre's work with African-Caribbean students. In this book one of his tutors, Julia Clarke, wrote that by all accounts, publishing was a good experience for Isaac. He received a lot of positive feedback from readers, including published reviews and correspondence and said that the process made him feel "more intelligent in myself because … plenty of people spoke to me about my book".[177] However, he was conflicted about the way his language was presented. While he wanted to retain control of the words he published, he also wanted the language he used to be "proper" English.[178]

Isaac wrote a second book on his own while the reading centre was closed for the summer. He worked as a park keeper in Hampstead Heath and asked a woman who swam every day in the bathing pools there to look at his writing. Isaac said: "She check it more so into 'proper' English, and my teacher didn't really please about how she put it into 'proper English', and I agree with my teacher too in that way, for I remember most of the other book everybody like how I speak, and that is how the teacher wrote it down as everybody did like it that way."[179] However, later in their conversation Isaac told Julia, his tutor, that "I would prefer the English", meaning standard English.[180] Chris O'Mahony, who with Jean Milloy worked with Isaac to prepare his second book, *It Can Happen*, for publication, thought that the tutors' political commitment to publishing students' writing in their own voices led them to disempower Isaac somewhat:

> He didn't like writing in his own vernacular, he really didn't, he wanted to write standard English, and of course we didn't want him to write standard English because we wanted his own voice. The corrected manuscript made absolute nonsense of his voice if you like. So we were kind of horrified, and, Jean and I had to try and persuade him, or force him, back into his own vernacular, which he really wasn't very happy about. But we did eventually produce a book, but he wasn't happy with it and neither was I really, I felt like we strong-armed him and that we didn't really listen to what he wanted. But the truth was, the book, the second book that he produced, was this woman from Hampstead pretending to be Isaac, and it wasn't him at all.
>
> And, it was a difficult thing. We weren't really smart enough to have the proper conversations with people about why it was important that they had their own language. They just felt a bit patronised by it I think, like we were kind of going, "There, there dear, your language is important."

Sue Shrapnel reflected that: "what stops it being acutely problematic is that, for most students, the technicalities are less important than the kinds of

[177] Schwab and Stone, *Language, Writing and Publishing: Work with Afro-Caribbean Students*, 30.
[178] Ibid.
[179] Ibid., 15.
[180] Ibid.

goodwill and attitude and the subtext that says, I think how you speak can be written down, is a stronger message than, woops, I fluffed, the [grammatical] niceties."[181] In some ways this seems to have been true for Isaac, who, leaving aside the controversy over language, said that he found the process of writing his second book (as opposed to dictating his first) to be a useful way of developing his own thinking about his life: "since I am able to write anything, I can understand it and I don't feel ashamed about it for I understand it clearer myself now."[182]

However, the use of students' own language to teach reading and writing was critiqued by some students and teachers. For instance, *Language, Writing and Publishing* quotes one black teacher, identified as "George" who says: "They don't have to come to you to learn to speak, they want to learn how to write things. I'm not saying you shouldn't teach them how to write in dialect but at the same time, the reason most of them want to, is not because they want just to write to friends, but some of them want not to feel left out of this society, and so putting them into a dialect mould isn't really helping them." A student put it more succinctly, "When I write a business letter, I don't want them to know from reading it I am West Indian. That way I won't get the attention I want."[183]

Jud argued the reading centre wasn't holding people back: "we had links with the college so that people could go on to more formal courses and get qualifications. It's important, I think, in second-chance education that there should be enough choice for people. So some of the people at the reading centre were never going to go on to another course, but if they had written their book that was a real achievement, and they may never have wanted to go and do something else." It wasn't that the reading centre didn't teach standard English, Irene explains, rather "we didn't always teach standard English", and the point at which to introduce it needed to be carefully judged for the individual pupil. In *Language Writing and Publishing* Jud and Irene recognised the imbalance of power involved in this decision: "It is rare that a student actually feels on an equal level with a tutor and it is actually a series of delicate negotiations, often with each side nudging the other to take decisions."[184] This seems to have been born out in Isaac's case, where decisions about the language he wrote in were made through protracted negotiation, but whether attempts to mitigate the teacher-taught power imbalance succeeded depended very much on the individual students and tutors involved.

We should be grateful

The publishing project, reading centre and bookshop all sought to provide a platform for writing by women and people from ethnic minorities, but an element of unease surrounded this work when it was carried out by workers who did not identify as being part of these groups. Oliver Flavin, who worked at Centerprise in the mid-1970s, says he questioned the role he

---

[181] Shrapnel, Interview with Sue Shrapnel (later Gardener) by Maggie Hewitt.

[182] Schwab and Stone, *Language, Writing and Publishing: Work with Afro-Caribbean Students*, 31.

[183] Ibid., 12.

[184] Ibid., 42.

An attempted jail break

Patience Agbabi performing at the Word Up Women's Café, early 1990s. Copyright © Sherlee Mitchell.

played, as a white man, in working with young black writers and increasing the bookshop's stock of African-Caribbean literature. Echoing the original idea of Centerprise as a catalyst for self-organised activity, he says "sometimes I felt like I was having to do things because I was the only person around who could do it, and that if there was a black person around who would take over from me, then fine. If something isn't being done, it may be appropriate to start doing it, and then if it sort of takes off, then, it can go off and look after itself, because, you know, some institution or some other people can continue it on and you don't have to do it anymore."

Whether workers were representative of the communities they served was an issue for all the projects within Centerprise. In the reading centre, the teacher/editor and student/writer power imbalance was complicated by the fact that the teachers were, for a long time, exclusively white while most students were African-Caribbean. Liesbeth de Block describes how, when she was working on *Every Birth It Comes Different* debates centred around "race and class … you know, who are you? a) you've never had children; b) you're white, c) you're middle class. I went to a private school. Who are you to come in and actually take control of a publication that's going to be presented as workers' writing, when you've done a lot of the work on it?" Sue Shrapnel described how in the 1970s the reading centre (entirely staffed by white tutors) tried to recruit black volunteers,[185] while Irene Schwab, who took over from Sue in 1981, says they tried to take action to ensure that "the profile of the workers should match the profile of our client body". Progress, however, was slow, although at least one black tutor, Terry Mentor, was employed in the 1980s. Jud says "I mean, it was always something that was problematic and not as Freire would have liked it. You were supposed, according to him, to match people by age, by race, by class."

As the publishing project consciously sought to increase the number of publications by writers from ethnic minority communities in the 1980s, the fact that the project was staffed entirely by white workers became increasingly contentious. In 1986 Maggie Hewitt and her co-worker Rebecca O'Rourke wrote a report on the publishing project's activities, stating that the last year had been "a struggle to keep going" with little support, they felt, from the wider collective. Concerns about the publishing project working with black writers had meant many books had been delayed, with only two published in 1985 to 1986. Maggie and Rebecca recommended that Centerprise employ a black worker to join the publishing project.[186]

The first black person to work in the publishing project, Michael McMillan, was hired the following year, in 1987. He was from Hackney and had been writing from a young age; his play *The School Leaver* was performed at the Royal Court when he was sixteen. He had been published by Black Ink press in Brixton, and attended their writing groups. At Centerprise he contributed to the production of *Not All Roses* (1987) by the Black Anthology Group, ran a weekly Black Writers Workshop out of which emerged the *Words, Sounds & Power* journal and received funding from Greater London Arts for his role

[185] Shrapnel, Interview with Sue Shrapnel (later Gardener) by Maggie Hewitt.

[186] Maggie Hewitt and Rebecca O'Rourke, 'Publishing Project Report', May 1986, A Hackney Autobiography, Bishopsgate Institute.

as a black literature worker. He feels that in some ways black writers were marginalised within the publishing project's approach, which he says was governed by an "old socialist idea of work and class" that did not consider black people to be part of the working class. He says "I questioned that, because, even at that point I was conscious of class. Well, we're part of the working class. I'm from a working-class background. I was clear about the distinctions. But I was aware that in a sense, unconsciously or consciously, it seemed as though black writers were seen as another class, or an underclass, somehow." Instead, Michael says he wanted black writers to be seen as "just writers who happen to be black".

Debates about Centerprise's working with black authors centred around certain publications produced in the mid-1980s. Particularly contentious was Pauline Wiltshire's award winning autobiography, *Living and Winning* (1985), which charts the struggle of its author to build an independent and fulfilling life despite the discrimination she had faced as a disabled black woman.[187] Pauline says she wrote the book because she was determined to challenge the way she was "treated like a little child", by the institutions she came into contact with and even some members of her own family. Publishing worker Maggie Hewitt worked with Pauline on her writing for around five years, supporting her to write by transcribing her words, reading them back to her and discussing editorial decisions. As *Living and Winning* was transcribed,

187
Living and Winning won the Socialist Bookfair's award for best popular history/autobiography in 1985. It was still one of Centerprise's bestselling publications in the early 1990s, when it was reprinted by publishing worker Bernadette Halpin.

Pauline Wiltshire (right) and Maggie Hewitt (left), working on a manuscript together in the offices upstairs at Centerprise, 1980s. Copyright © Ingrid Pollard.

like Isaac Gordon's first book, it was mediated through another person. This way of working meant there was particular potential for misunderstandings and disagreements to arise between the writer and editor. In Maggie's introduction to *Living and Winning* she wrote that they had "argued … for hours" about the place of religion in the book, for instance.[188] Pauline describes in her interview disagreeing with Maggie about half way through the process, when she felt it was being turned from a "black book" into an "English book". Pauline feels she successfully asserted what she wanted with the support of other black people and was happy with the final version. She has since published another memoir, *Legs of Iron* (2011).

The book *Wesley My Only Son*, published in 1987, was written by Monica Jules to share her experience of bringing up her autistic son as a single mother. Monica Jules was a reading centre student and African-Caribbean. The black writers' group the Words, Sounds and Power Writers' Workshop wrote to Centerprise that they "felt incensed, disappointed and mortified at the way the book has been presented."[189] It was the introduction, in which Monica Jules and Jud Stone, the tutor who had worked with Monica, were interviewed about the process of creating the book, that drew Words, Sounds and Power's ire; they felt that it had patronised the author. Like in other Centerprise publications, the introduction was intended to make the publishing process more transparent, partly as a resource to encourage similar community publishing to happen elsewhere. Michael McMillan, one of the signatories to the letter, says now that in his opinion "the way that black writing or black writers had been published, it was a bit paternalistic, in a way. They weren't really involved in the publishing process. It was like an afterthought on some level. Centerprise had published some black work, but I wondered how much, in encountering that black work, it had transformed Centerprise itself."

The reading centre and publishing project tried to encourage writers and students to take part in the publishing process, although each book was generally co-ordinated by one or more of the workers. In the introduction to the reading centre publication *Every Birth It Comes Different* tutors Liesbeth de Block, Jud Stone and Aydin Mehmet Ali wrote: "It became clear to the three of us, that our role was to be the co-ordinators of the project and as far as possible let decisions be made by the group of writers." They describe the "first production meeting" when students enthusiastically chose the photos and titles "with cries of 'yes' or 'no'", as well as a Saturday session when "everyone was invited to have a go at laying out some pages."[190] While some writers were keen to get involved in all aspects of making their books, Liesbeth reflects that for some it was "quite the reverse, 'You know how to do it; you do it,' you know? 'It's your job; do it.' I think it was an incredible expectation that people would come in and do these things, they had their own lives. So, in a way, the class thing came in in our expectations of their participation." Monica Jules hints at this tension in the introduction to her book, making it clear that her priority was to work quickly and produce the

---

[188] Pauline Wiltshire, *Living and Winning* (London: Centerprise, 1985), 6.

[189] Words, Sounds & Power Writers' Workshop, 'Words, Sounds & Power Writers' Workshop Letter to Centerprise on Wesley My Only Son', n.d., A Hackney Autobiography, Bishopsgate Institute.

[190] Hackney Reading Centre, *Every Birth It Comes Different*, 7.

book as a resource for other parents: "we do no messing about ... I want it to finish ... because I got so much at the moment to do."[191]

As discussed above, writing workshops, with their group editorial processes, were seen as a way to resolve some of the power imbalance between writers and editors. Another alternative way of producing publications can be seen in the production of *Breaking the Silence* (1984), a groundbreaking collection of writing by Asian women, with each account presented in both English and the writer's language. Importantly, it was not Centerprise's project, the idea came from the Dalston Children's Centre collective. The book was developed by Manju Mukherjee, with the photographer Anna Sherwin, both of whom worked at Dalston Children's Centre. After their initial idea to host a group for young women at the centre didn't work out, Manju met women out shopping, at the school gates, parks and bus stops, and convinced them to write their stories, often anonymously. The women wrote about coming to the UK, about arranged marriage and racism, and parents who expected their UK born daughters "to be like a girl born in Karachi or Bombay, instead of an apple expecting a mango."[192] Manju and Anna approached Centerprise for help publishing the book. This, the publishing project wrote in a preface, was a new experience "where we were more of a resource to be drawn on than directors of the project [which] will stand us in good stead for future collaborations."[193]

Breaking the Silence was not, however, without controversy: Manju says she was criticised after the book was published for working with a non-Asian photographer. Maggie and Rebecca invited some of the critics to discuss the issues with Manju and when the book was followed up by an exhibition, *Aurat Shakti*, this was produced by a team of Asian women, including Manju and one of the women who had negatively reviewed *Breaking the Silence*, without the involvement of Centerprise.[194] Maggie and Rebecca wrote: "We felt this was a positive experience for us, in that criticisms were aired and discussed in a way that made it possible for the group to move forward very positively to something else."[195] *Breaking the Silence* was different from the normal way Centerprise worked, but while Manju and Anna were co-producers working in partnership with the publishing project, the women whose stories were published in the book were, by necessity, anonymous and distanced from the production process.[196]

While writers were encouraged to participate as much as possible in the work of publishing, they were expected to do so without pay. As in similar community publishing projects elsewhere, writers retained the copyright to their work but any money Centerprise made from sales was ploughed back into the project to publish the next person's writing. Ken Worpole's report on the first five years of the project bluntly stated "We do not pay authors. We see this kind of local publishing as a service we offer and share with people as part of developing a common local culture. To begin paying fees and royalties could begin to encourage the professionalism of writing."[197] To some the policy of not paying writers for their work must have contrasted sharply

---

[191] Monica Jules, *Wesley, My Only Son* (London: Centerprise, 1987), 7.

[192] Centerprise Trust Ltd and Dalston Children's Centre, eds., *Breaking the Silence* (London: Centerprise Trust in association with Dalston Children's Centre, 1984), 2.

[193] Centerprise Trust Ltd and Dalston Children's Centre, *Breaking the Silence* Preface.

[194] Publishing Project report 1986.

[195] Ibid.

[196] Two of the women whose writing was published in *Breaking the Silence* published their stories under their own names, the rest did so under pseudonyms.

[197] Worpole, *Local Publishing & Local Culture*, 17.

Eveline Marius, a writer published by Centerprise, 1980s. Photograph courtesy of Maggie Hewitt.

with the salaries paid to Centerprise workers. One of the young writers, Eveline Marius, told doctoral student Birgit Harris: "A lot of the time you're left to feel we should be grateful that we published it, you know – patronising. That's what a lot of black writers feel, that they're being patronised."[198] Eveline argued that the publishing project should increase the price charged for books and use the extra money as a fund for writers who were struggling, or to help them attend events, for instance, but it is unclear whether her recommendations were put into practice.

In 1986 Sue Shrapnel commented to Birgit Harris: "The workshop(s) and Centerprise have made space for women and for black writers when those spaces were hard to come by. But times change. Some of what black writers want to say they must say without us [white people]."[199] As time went on it became increasingly possible to find books by women and ethnic minority writers in all bookshops, not only in alternative or community shops like Centerprise. Eva Lewin, who worked at the literature development project from 1994, remembers book launches at Centerprise in the 1990s "when a whole bunch of new black writers were starting to be published, and there was just this hunger for black writers." It became easier, but by no means easy enough, for a more diverse range of writers to gain recognition and be published. Still, many of the people supported to write and publish by

[198] Harris, 'The Federation of Worker Writers and Community Publishers – Gemeinde Arbeit Und Identitätsbildung', 210.

[199] Ibid., 237.

Centerprise would never have done so if left to the vagaries of commercial publishers. As Ken Worpole wrote in 1977:

> Yet even if Centerprise collapsed tomorrow, it is reassuring to think that in many homes, in front rooms, on bookshelves or on mantelpieces there would remain pieces of tangible evidence that the people who live in Hackney have a history, have written about themselves, have tried to describe and understand the world they have lived in, and which they have wanted to share with others.[200]

[200] Worpole, *Local Publishing & Local Culture*, 20.

Chris O'Mahony (left) and Maggie Hewitt (right) knitting, 1980s. Photograph courtesy of Maggie Hewitt.

5: The collective

The only way to work

Centerprise's founders planned it to be managed collectively by both its workers and the wider community. They were determined to be different from the Hoxton Café Project, where well-to-do trustees controlled the project at a distance, alienated from those who worked at and used the project by both geography and class. Toby Taper wrote in her report on Centerprise's first three years: "It was central to the whole concept … that it must succeed or fail as a community project within a specified time period, so everyone involved in its setting up – workers and trustees alike – would pledge themselves to leave at the end of three years by which time it must either be able to run without them or it would close."[201] Taking over from the charity's board of trustees in 1973, a large group of local residents – "the Centerprise Co-op" – met regularly for discussions, drawing in some of the people involved in the various projects connected to Centerprise, such as Hackney Playbus and *Hackney People's Press*, into the management of the organisation. A smaller group drawn from the larger co-op, the "Centerprise Council" met regularly to make strategic decisions, and yet another body, the Council of Management was elected annually from amongst the membership to take formal legal responsibility for the organisation.

While in theory answerable to the wider co-op, the workers organised themselves as a collective and had a great deal of autonomy in day-to-day management. The Centerprise Co-op newsletter in March/April 1974 reassured members that the workers' collective wasn't "a secret society meeting, whatever it might seem like" and invited members to come and sit in on meetings if they wanted.[202] The division of responsibility between the co-op and the collective was, however, not immediately clear. On 30 September 1974 an extraordinary meeting was called for the co-op to discuss what their "rights and duties" were and how that fitted in with the workers' collective. The meeting announcement hoped for a "rousing discussion" and a "large stroppy crowd".[203]

From its opening in 1971 until it moved to the high street in 1974, Centerprise had functioned "like a partnership of workers operating separate projects within the same building."[204] Glenn Thompson, the pivotal figure of the early years tended to encourage people to do their own thing, without seeking to micromanage or control them. His first wife and Centerprise co-founder, Margaret Gosley says "If you had an idea and he thought it was good, he expected you to do it." This perhaps helps to explain the astonishing plethora of activity generated in such a short time period, as the workers, Glenn included, were not prevented from carrying out their ideas. However, only confident and fairly experienced workers coped well in an environment

[201] Taper, 'Report on the First Three Years'.

[202] Centerprise Trust Ltd, 'Centerprise Newsletter March/April 1974', 1974, Arts Council of Great Britain Archive.

[203] Centerprise Trust Ltd, 'Announcement of a Special Meeting at Centerprise on Monday 30 September 1974', 1974, Arts Council of Great Britain Archive.

[204] Centerprise Trust Ltd, 'Centerprise Annual Report 1978.'

where you were expected to sink or swim without much support.

The workers met on Monday mornings for brief, business-like meetings. Still, community worker Anthony Kendall remembers, with Glenn, being frustrated that time in meetings was wasted on "the changing a bulb syndrome, you spend four hours debating whose role it was to do that, rather than just bloody well getting on and doing it." Ken Worpole describes a similar attitude to the collective with a different emphasis, reflecting that he was generally "in favour of collectivity", but did not want to describe the mechanics of how the collective worked, as that would digress from what he found much more interesting to discuss: "the zeitgeist and the politics of this movement of community bookshops, community publishing."

On Kingsland High Street, after many of the first group of workers had left, the collective rethought the management structure and distributed responsibility more broadly across the group of workers. The early emphasis on reaching outwards to spark activity shifted towards a slightly more inward focus on process and how things got done. As advice worker Janet Rees who started work in 1979 remembers, "we talked a lot about the collective, we were a very self-conscious collective." Collective management, Centerprise wrote in 1978, "is a political statement in itself, prefiguring and demonstrating the possibility of forms of working life and social organisation that give hope for a future state of society."[205] The people involved were often already ensconced within a wider radical culture that encouraged collectivity, organising their housing through communes or squats and their childcare through co-operatives. Jean Milloy, commenting on starting work at Centerprise in 1979 without much prior experience of collectives, quipped "it was the 1970s, I was prepared to be a bit alternative", while Rosie Ilett who joined Centerprise in 1984 explains that "working in a collective was just how you did things" in radical organisations:

> **Because that's what you thought was the right way to be inclusive, democratic, to make decisions that brought everybody's views in, to represent a diversity, all of that kind of thing. … And within also a very politicised funding environment. That was the days of the GLC, Greater London Arts Alliance, that required lots of these structures and ways of behaving to almost be part of how they funded you. So there was really a very big need for those kind of ways of working to be a part of it. And there were a lot of people, probably me included at the time, that felt that was the only way to work.**

Collective decision-making was an ambitious structure for a complex, multifaceted project like Centerprise to adopt. Most co-operatives had a single, or main focus, for instance they might be a bookshop. The members of such a co-op would share both the experience of working in their bookshop and a sense of common purpose. At Centerprise multiple but interconnected projects shared a building and pooled their finances. Collective members were expected to make decisions about areas of work beyond their ex-

[205] Ibid.

pertise, which was time-consuming, and, Jean Milloy says, required "a lot of care". Dorothea Smartt, black arts worker in the early 1990s explains: "somebody who worked in the bookshop or the café had a say about what went on in the publishing project, without necessarily having the insight [required], in the same way that I wouldn't necessarily have insight into what was going on in the youth project or the advice centre." Janet remembers feeling duty bound to intelligently question the other projects: "So that if the publishing project said, 'We want to publish 2,000 copies of *An Austrian Cockney*,' where do you begin to be the challenge to that? If you've walked in, if you're twenty-five and you've just been in advice centre work all your life, how do you make a sensible contribution to that? It's not necessarily a straightforward thing. I got in the habit of asking questions about storage. 'Well where are you going to put all these books?' Sound as if I'd thought about it. You had to think of an angle that you could pursue."

The workers' Monday meetings began to take up more and more time. Meanwhile, the shops were shut for the day, allowing the workers to meet and then clean the building together. The long meetings could be frustrating, "hard, hard, hard", as Irene Schwab says. They could also be "exciting", Chris O'Mahony relates, while Janet describes her attitude to the meeting being one of "total respect" for the collective decision-making process. Rosie explains that the meetings were important because:

> Most people in Centerprise worked with the public. So, you couldn't be having a catch-up chat with people about, oh we need to plan that, at the same time as working with the public … So, there was clearly a need to have this protected space to [make decisions] but, it was very, very lengthy and laborious. I mean I can remember being in the meetings, and sometimes just a sort of, level of frustration … But also excitement. I mean, I'm sounding a bit negative. Obviously you bring together people with lots of different ideas, there were people that perhaps only worked part-time, you didn't see them as much, that was really good. You know, you got a sense of what was going on.

All the workers took turns to chair the meetings and take minutes and each worker would report back about their projects, raise any issues they faced and receive feedback from the wider group. Irene explains:

> There were things called personal reports where you had to talk about what you felt about what had been going on, which were pretty excruciating a lot of the time. Some people let their hearts out as it were, and some didn't.[206]
>
> And sometimes there were the bigger issues, like, where are we going, and what are we doing, and are we doing the right thing, and, equality issues. There were also the very nitty-gritty, small ones like post that's come in, visitors, who's going to take them round. And, then there were things like particular clients or cus-

[206] In a proposal to the collective titled "What's Happened to Caring?" written in June 1983 Irene and Chris describe the personal report system used in collective meetings: "one is supposed to air one's feelings about one's work and relationships with the other members of the collective. Unfortunately the group is now so large that it's very difficult to express any personal emotions in front of so large a number of people. Also, the fact that there is no feedback from others when making a personal report means that you may have just bared your soul to be left feeling 'high and dry' by a bunch of silent strangers."

tomers, who had been badly behaved in some way, should we ban them. And we had to make a decision on things, and there had to be pretty much a consensus.

Claudia remembers: "They were quite fiery meetings, because there was no hierarchy, and often egos would get involved. They were very dramatic. And, sometimes things would go on in the meetings that you just couldn't quite believe. It could be like a sort of theatre, you could be entertained by it. I was nineteen years old and it was my first experience in the workplace, and it's like, ever since, I've worked in other places, everything's sort of closed. So if someone sexually harassed someone else, only the people involved will know. But because we did everything together, if someone did something like touch someone else's bum, everyone would know about it, and we'd all have a go at them in the meeting. And it was just completely, not like anywhere else."

All workers were paid on the same scale, according to their outgoings, such as how many dependants they had, rather than their area of responsibility. A system of "work-sharing" meant that each worker did weekly shifts in the bookshop, coffee bar, public office (acting as receptionists and operating the switchboard) as well as sharing the collective tasks like cleaning the toilets, feeding the cats and opening up in the mornings. Workers could also choose to do shifts in other projects, helping out in a supporting role in the advice centre, publishing project or reading centre, for instance. Some, like Chris O'Mahony, "liked the variety" work-sharing provided but it did mean there was less time to focus on their main roles. Jean Milloy turned up for her first day of work in the bookshop on a Monday morning in 1979 and was "completely gobsmacked" to find herself "nowhere near the bookshop", instead spending her first day embroiled in a meeting, followed by the weekly collective cleaning session. In 1979 workers only had two days in the week to focus on their own area of responsibility, spending the rest of their forty-five hour week on collective responsibilities. Balancing this demanding schedule could be difficult. Maggie Hewitt reported on her first three months in post: "it's easiest if I work one of my four shifts a day but that means that all my publishing project time gets broken up, so I try to work shifts together to give me at least one day clear for publishing work."[207]

1970s collectivist culture encouraged work-sharing systems as a way of challenging hierarchy; preventing individuals from dominating because of their skills and knowledge by making everyone spend some time outside of their specialisms.[208] At Centerprise it was also intended to make all the workers, especially those who worked upstairs, in the advice centre, reading centre and publishing project, more accessible to local people. The shopfronts put the work of the collective on display. Potentially this could make workers feel they were "on the frontline" and "exposed", as Jean says, although Wendy Pettifer, advice worker, remembers "a lot of our advice centre clients would hang out in the coffee bar and it created a really good atmos-

A Centerprise cat, 1980s. Photograph courtesy of Maggie Hewitt.

[207] Hewitt, 'Maggie's Three Month Review.'

[208] A. Stanton, 'Citizens of Workplace Democracies', Critical Social Policy 9, no. 26 (1 September 1989): 56–65.

phere, made them feel more relaxed, more open, there was a lot of mixing of age, race, class, sex." Janet Rees describes how advice centre customers could nab them without having to queue up at the drop-in times, often telling them "really important personal things when you were buttering the bread for the sandwiches". She concludes: "It was good that we were so visible, I think it's good that there was no mystique. If we had been like the bureaucrats, then, we would have just been other bureaucrats, and they would have been cut off from the process. I mean the fact that the process was so visible to them, that we were so visible and accessible, I think, all of that was a good thing. And, the fact that they saw us mopping the floor at the end of the night, and being on the till, I think that was good. Because, what we were trying to demonstrate is that you just needed a bit of knowledge, that these were rights, that anyone could do this."

Pam Toussaint (right) and Pat in the coffee bar, c. 1981. Photograph courtesy of Wendy Pettifer.

In 1978 Centerprise wrote that behind work-sharing was "a commitment to breaking down conventional assumptions about sex roles, which might have left us with women working in the coffee bar, and men doing the managing; and about the relative values of manual and intellectual work."[209] Publishing workers were especially liable to come under criticism for considering their work to be "intellectually superior." Bernadette Halpin, publishing worker in the early 1990s, says "there was always a bit of a whiff of being a bit intellectual, and a bit snotty, and that dreaded thing, middle class.

[209] Centerprise Trust Ltd, 'Centerprise Annual Report 1978.'

Although these things weren't necessarily said. It was said to me, 'What, are you too good to come and cook in the café?' I said, 'No. I just couldn't cook in the café.'" The idea that anyone could cook in the café, staff the bookshop or clean the building, in a sense maintained a distinction between manual and intellectual work, devaluing the former. In reality not all workers had the requisite skills to do these jobs well, as Neil Martinson says: "I cooked chilli con carne every bloody week, because I didn't know how to cook anything else." Bookshop worker Rosie Ilett was frustrated by the idea that just anyone could work as a bookseller and feels that bookshop sales suffered as a result of unskilled staff: "you might be very politically committed to Centerprise, and very committed to collective working, and really support it and live in Hackney and think it was fantastic, but if you're looking for a book, and you go in there on a Saturday or any other day, and the person looks at you as if they don't know what you're talking about, why would you go in there?"

Work-sharing, with the requirement to know several very different areas of work well, added pressure to an already intense workload. As Janet said: "your head would burst from all the things you had to know". In Wendy Pettifer's three-month report given to the collective in 1980, she critiqued what she'd found to be "the unspoken expectation that staff should work more than 45 hours" and advocated improved working conditions "because [the workload] leads to staff being tense, tired and unable to present an "open" face to the public, as well as competition as to who is the most dedicated, committed worker."[210] Janet remembers working at Centerprise as all-encompassing. When she worked elsewhere she had been involved in feminist and trade union activity, but once at Centerprise: "It absolutely took over our lives, well it certainly took over my life. One day somebody asked me where we slept, because they assumed that we slept upstairs somewhere. We were just always there. It was like joining a monastic order, except that you could still have sex, but apart from that, it was like being in a community away from the world. Well, one of those groups that serves the communities, out in the community."

Rosie Ilett says that generally, "people got on very well, people often used to go out after work for a drink." Friendships developed, both amongst the workers and with and between the writers, volunteers, students and customers. Amongst the collective, Jean Milloy describes that the intensity of the work could result in particularly strong friendships being formed. Some met their long-term partners through working at Centerprise and there were many shorter-lived flings. Workers often shared communal housing, or worked together in other initiatives outside of Centerprise. This complex web of relationships blurred boundaries between work and home, and what was going on in people's personal lives – who was sleeping with who, who had fallen out – couldn't help but influence dynamics in the wider collective.

Wendy reflects that the collective maintained quite a strict structure for the workers and monitored what hours they worked. Janet describes their style of collective management as the opposite of "he without sin should cast the

[210] Wendy Pettifer, 'Wendy Pettifer's Report to the Centerprise Collective for Her Three-Month Review', 1980, A Hackney Autobiography, Bishopsgate Institute.

Maggie Hewitt in the coffee bar kitchen, tired after a shift, June 1981. The photographer wrote a poem to accompany the print, "Unposed Photograph". Photograph courtesy of Maggie Hewitt.

first stone. We didn't believe that, we very explicitly did not believe in that. We went out of our way to say you were able to lay into someone else even if you were guilty of similar crimes." Maggie says it was more challenging than a traditional, hierarchical structure to work in: "because people could see what you were doing, or what you weren't doing, and therefore challenge other people. So you were held to account very often if people didn't like things and so on. In a way people could comment on whatever they liked, because it was a collective." Bernadette remembers her first collective meeting, in 1990, when: "there was a woman really getting quite beaten up by the rest of the table. There was that terrible thing that can happen in collectives where everybody's under stress, and people can get scapegoated. I can clearly remember sitting in that very first meeting, thinking to myself, 'I don't want to be here.' The collective spirit at that meeting was awful, and I do distinctly remember thinking to myself – a bit like when you meet someone and you think 'I want to be in a relationship with this person but I shouldn't' – I remember sitting in that meeting thinking, I really want this job, and I didn't have a job, but I had never seen anything like it, I have to say, I had never been in a meeting like that."

Centerprise workers cooking together on a weekend away, Darsham, Suffolk, 1980s. From left to right: Ruth Bashall, Wendy Pettifer, Sarah Morrison. Photograph courtesy of Wendy Pettifer.

There was a strong emphasis on holding each other to account, but less on providing support. Janet says that if the collective was providing line management, "Mr Grumpy was our line manager". Collective scrutiny may have been intense but it was at times unevenly applied. In 1981 it transpired that a number of vital funding applications had simply not been made. The financial shortfall that ensued meant that five out of ten jobs were temporarily lost. There was not enough money to keep up the same level of activity, no new books were published or even purchased for the shop and the building only stayed open because of the efforts of its workers, volunteers and supporters, who raised money and ran the shops voluntarily.[211] Jean identifies that the problem was "nobody was interested in book-keeping, apart from the bookkeeper, and nobody bothered to find out what was going on. ... things got sorted out in the end. But even within a collective, there are certain jobs that people don't want to know about, and that was one. And that was a bit sad. ... It wasn't seen as an area, like the coffee bar or the bookshop. It wasn't tangible." Janet remembers that in the end she "quite liked the crisis" because as a consequence they all pulled together and came to better understand the finances.

The workers' collective, with its time-consuming and inward-focused structure, was the real centre of power in the organisation. The collective did not include most of the people who worked at Centerprise, primarily because it would have taken too much time for part-time workers or volunteers to participate in the weekly meetings. As local people were often employed as sessional or part-time workers, this meant the collective was

[211] Centerprise Trust Ltd, 'Centerprise Annual Report 1982.'

generally less representative of the community around Centerprise than the total sum of the people who worked there were. In general, the collective did not reflect, in terms of its class and ethnic makeup, the people who used the building, and neither, at times, did the Council of Management. This meant, Janet remembers, that during the time she worked at Centerprise (1979 to 1985), the workers told the Council of Management as little as possible and ignored their recommendations. The resulting lack of oversight perhaps contributed to the financial crisis of 1981. Janet says: "These were lovely people who were hugely committed to making Hackney a better place to live and have all sorts of fantastic attributes. They were clever, and knowledgeable about how organisations worked. I think if they'd been more representative of our users, certainly our advice centre users and our reading centre users, we would not have treated them with so little respect, I think we would have treated them with a great deal more respect, and given them the tools they needed to do the job."

Within the workers' collective some experienced there to be a dominant, if informal, hierarchy. Wendy wrote, three months into her post, that she found the meetings to be intimidating and alienating.[212] When interviewed, she commented that the people who had been there longest, the "more confident, better-educated characters" tended to dominate. She says: "I think I just found [the collective] quite frustrating really because I didn't perceive myself as one of those characters." Michael McMillan, a publishing worker from 1987 to 1989, considers that hierarchy permeated Centerprise, effectively excluding black people from positions of power: "There was a power base that was already there, and did not involve anybody of colour." Rosie described how when she started work in 1984, there was already an "old guard", part of the "post-hippy" generation of the early seventies that had "done very radical things in their time". She considers that lack of a clear structure can perpetuate informal hierarchies: "There is nothing structureless about structurelessness.[213] There is always going to be something there, and it's going to be invisible, and people don't acknowledge it, and that's part of the problem. It's actually better to say there is a structure, and there are people that have slightly different roles."

Irene describes how when she started work in 1981: "there were a lot of arguments around gender and sexuality, how can we make ourselves more accessible, to women, lesbian, gay, bisexual people, and so on. And that gradually gave way to more arguments about race and ethnicity, and how could we be more accessible for the black and ethnic minority community in Dalston." Janet Rees said that when she started work in 1979:

> We, the collective, were entirely white, the groups we worked with were very mixed in ethnicity, and we tried to address issues of inequality, in the bookshop, in the groups we supported … we were alert to the issues, and we made some efforts to try to recruit black and ethnic minority people in particular where the gap between us and the community we were serving was so enormous and so

[212] Pettifer, 'Wendy Pettifer's Report to the Centerprise Collective for Her Three-Month Review'.

[213] Rosie is referring to ideas contained in *The Tyranny of Structurelessness* by Jo Freeman, an article first published in 1972 in *The Second Wave*.

obvious. We did during the time I was there appoint some black staff, and that was a huge step forward for us, but we were still not reflecting the community around us. ... Sorry, I'm folding my arms defensively here, I do feel shifty about it. I mean, when I started we were entirely white, when I left we were, more representative of the community we served, but not very representative. We were white and young actually, is what we were, and, graduates. And, we were slightly different by the time I left.

Chris describes the decision to confront racism in the collective as "a key event". She says "we began to notice that the kind of lower status jobs were black people's jobs, or people who did hours in the café but [were] not collective members [were black]." Michael McMillan, the first black person to work in the publishing project, did not feel supported at Centerprise: "It wasn't as if the organisation were completely behind what I was trying to do. It was somehow tolerated, I hate that word tolerated, but, it was somehow, oh well he's doing his thing, let him get on with it. But it wasn't really embraced, as something that could benefit Centerprise." Michael describes how things came to a head when:

> After [I'd been in post] about eighteen months, I had accumulated so much toil [time off in lieu] that for the next year I could take off every Friday. At the time, I wanted to do a part-time MA in independent film and video at Central Saint Martins. I raised it as an issue, that I wanted to do it, but I had already signed up, so I wasn't asking them, I was telling them, this is what I want to do. Because for me, my education's more important than the job. I had already started. And they said, "No, you can't do it." I said, "I'm doing it anyway. I'm doing it anyway."

After a difficult period, when he was suspended from his post, Michael was eventually dismissed from Centerprise. He reflects that although his time at Centerprise was personally stressful, it may have been "pivotal to the shift that took place" within the organisation. From Michael's time onwards there was always a black arts worker or black literature development worker (a role he had created) at Centerprise. Claudia Manchanda, who worked in the coffee bar from 1989, said that "when I was there, most of the people that went to Centerprise, and most of the workers, were black and Asian, with I think one or two white workers. And I think there was a transition politically and culturally of the organisation that was happening around that time of the '80s. So, it was a safe place for people of colour to be in, and had a very rich Caribbean culture within it."

There was an unspoken expectation that workers would treat their employment as more than a job. When Michael explicitly prioritised his personal development: "my education is more important than the job", he clashed with this culture. In some ways, this was a vestige of the 1970s, a part of the Centerprise legacy that stretched back to the seventy-hour working week of the first three years. Ken Worpole describes being "shocked when people coming to work at Centerprise said they didn't think the wages were high enough, because at the time, I thought you should work for nothing more or less. Because we weren't working, we were making social change. The fact is, I did need to earn money, but the idea that people should think seriously about money and pensions and all that, I found that quite difficult." To some extent this attitude persisted into the 1990s; Bernadette remembers "a real seriousness, gravity, you know, about how we lived our lives, and what we were about", and Dorothea describes their "commitment to collectivism, and trying to find new ways of working together. It didn't always work but there was a commitment there to moving away from capitalism, actively trying to do things differently." Workers often left Centerprise after deciding they needed more time for their personal lives. As Robin Simpson, who was generally very positive about his time at Centerprise, says "you can't carry on doing everything till one o'clock in the morning, people have lives to live." By the time Irene was ready to leave in 1990, she says, she "just wanted to have a boss! I didn't want to be in charge of anything anymore."

Many of the workers went on to very successful careers in diverse fields, often building on experience gained at Centerprise. At the time, however, the collective actively sought to prevent workers gaining too much individual prestige from their work, as Janet explains:

> One of the things that was pushed at the collective meetings was to make it impossible for a Centerprise worker to become famous through working at Centerprise. We were very antagonistic to the idea that the individuals who worked there could make a name for themselves. So, it was always about pushing the users, the ordinary people of Hackney who used our services, to the front, always, always. So, when the *London Programme* came to do this hour-long session [on the Smalley Road housing campaign], I was absolutely forbidden by the collective from appearing in the programme, even though I knew all the people, I knew the story. Because, it wasn't seen to be appropriate, it was seen to be downright dangerous for there to be any sort of, personality politics around the people in Centerprise. So, I sort of understood that, it made sense to me, I accepted it, but it reminded me of my childhood in Wales and being a Baptist, you know, you work hard, you're very self-effacing, you're very modest, you put yourself to the back of the queue. It was all those sorts of values that were imbued with it.

In the background of how Janet describes the collective seems to be a distinction between the workers and "the ordinary people of Hackney". For people leaving better paid, professional jobs to work at Centerprise, to earn less money and work more hours, there was an element of conscious self-sacrifice in their decision to do so. After fifteen years of teaching,

Maggie started work at Centerprise and "the salary was half what I had been earning. And my colleagues at school thought I was having a nervous breakdown, I was completely mad, because that's something nobody ever does really." It wasn't all self-sacrifice and gloom, there were many benefits to working in the collective. Some of the terms and conditions of the collective set themselves were generous, such as the maternity package of six months off work at full pay, followed by six months at half pay. People could generally bring their children into work with them when childcare arrangements failed. Irene remembered her twins drawing on the very bottom of the whiteboard while she taught her students on days their nursery was closed. For others, often those who were young at the time, working at Centerprise was a step up in terms of pay and responsibility. Barbara Schulz, Claudia Manchanda and Neil Martinson, all worked at Centerprise from very young ages, and felt that by doing so they accessed responsibilities and experiences they may not have found elsewhere.

Both Barbara and Claudia describe taking part in the collective management of Centerprise as life changing. Barbara says as it was her "first experience of life", collective organisation became "the norm" for her and "I've never been able to get out of that really. I still find hierarchy agonising; it irritates the hell out of me." Claudia echoes this sentiment: "Nowhere ever seemed to ever come close to working at Centerprise. I always felt hard done by wherever I worked afterwards. And I always begrudged being ordered around. I didn't know what an amazing place it was, and that I actually was autonomous, with Erita. Even though I used to dread some of the Monday meetings, I didn't realise how lucky I was and privileged to work somewhere where we ran a whole organisation. And that my opinion, or someone else's opinion, could affect another project even, or give it a wonderful idea. You actually felt important in a process."

Workers thought, at the time and when they were interviewed, about how the collective could have been improved. The individual projects could have had more independence, the meetings could have been shorter and there could have been kinder support and supervision procedures in place. A proposal made by Chris and Irene in 1983 entitled "What's happened to caring?" suggested there be a system of small support groups, meeting every other week to offer a supportive environment for staff to discuss their work and any issues they were experiencing.[214] Rosie Ilett reflects that an underlying problem was the collective's insistence that everyone must be "seen as being the same", when people had different qualifications, levels of experience and knowledge. The problem, she says is "how you include everybody, and how you make things really diverse and inclusive, whilst recognising that people bring all sorts of things to that" including different levels of skill, experience, interest and need to be involved. Some collective members may not have had a high level of formal education, but they may have been better equipped in some ways to run Centerprise, where so much of the work involved dealing successfully with other people. Having raised several

[214] Irene Schwab and Chris O'Mahony, 'What's Happened to Caring?', June 1983, A Hackney Autobiography, Bishopsgate Institute.

children, or recently having been an angry teenager yourself, for instance, made you better qualified to decide what to do about young people acting disruptively in the coffee bar, than someone else's university degree.[215] The collective aimed for all the workers to contribute on an equal footing. It was an imperfect attempt, but it seems likely that many of those involved in the collective had more power and influence than they would have had within a hierarchical system of management.

The collective ends

By the end of the decade Centerprise faced an uncertain future of austerity and funding cuts. The GLC was abolished by the Thatcher government in 1986 and the ILEA in 1990. Initially projects and organisations that had been funded by the GLC were transferred to the newly created London Boroughs Grants Committee (LGBC). This body was given a budget by central government which was smaller than that originally proposed during the dissolution of the GLC. As an inter-borough body, representatives from Conservative boroughs were able to oppose the funding of "a large number of groups servicing women, black and ethnic minorities and gays and lesbians."[216] Hackney Council shouldered the burden of funding those local organisations that were left struggling, including Centerprise, and as a result its own grant-making budgets became increasingly tight. From 1988 onwards Hackney Council began making cuts to its grants budget, making a reduction of 7.5 per cent that year.[217] Central government policies of the later 1980s and early 1990s also pushed Hackney to reduce the support it gave to community organisations. In 1990 local authorities were restricted to spending just £5 per head of population on grant-funding charitable groups, forcing a 30 per cent cut in Hackney's total grants budget.[218] In 1991 Centerprise's grant from Hackney Council's Leisure Services was cut by £4,000, while the rent set by the Council was raised by £14,000.[219] The closure of Hackney Under Fives, which had lost its funding in January 1991, meant Centerprise lost a further £2,000 in revenue. This meant that Centerprise was losing at least £20,000, which was in 1991 almost 23 per cent of its total income. A leaflet produced by Centerprise predicted this would mean "the complete closure of all services within two or three years".[220]

In 1990 Centerprise had appointed a new administrator, Neil Barklem, who had responsibility for finance and fundraising. Unlike the other workers, who worked within specific projects, the administrator had a centralised role, overseeing the financing, administration and upkeep of the building. In just his first month Neil was given the task of compiling a three-year development plan for Centerprise. After six weeks in post Neil wrote in his report to the collective that "with a rapid turnover of staff in recent years the place seems to be lacking a shared identity and direction for the future."[221] A few weeks later, he suggested that "the collective needs to adapt to the demands of the 1990s in its working patterns", adding he felt "very strongly that a four

Demonstration in support of Centerprise outside Hackney Town Hall, 1981. Phil "Eddie" Edwards (first from right), Ken Worpole (second from right), Guy Farrar (fourth from right), Larraine Worpole (fifth from right), Janet Rees (standing, fifth from left), and Andrew Roberts (second from left). Image courtesy of London Borough of Hackney Archives.

hour weekly meeting gives more negative results psychologically then it does in terms of efficiency or management of the organisation."[222] In Centerprise's Annual Report of 1991, Neil wrote that in line with Hackney Council's new funding priorities, he planned to increase the amount of self-generated income and reduce dependence on grants. There was a need, Neil wrote, to improve Centerprise's "Public Relations" with Hackney Council and other funders, alongside developing a "corporate image".[223] This shift in language towards terms resonant of market capitalism departs from Centerprise's earlier reports, from the contemplative idealism of the 1970s, to the defiance of the 1980s, which asserted "We Shall Not Close" in the face of Thatcherite cuts.[224]

1992, the year Centerprise celebrated its twenty-first anniversary, was described in the Chair's report as a "difficult year". Some small increases of funding had come in, including £9,000 from Hackney Leisure Services, but the money had stipulations attached to "improve the efficiency of our service delivery and build on our business capacity."[225] The new posts of centre manager and bookshop manager, it was hoped, would deliver this greater efficiency. Neil Barklem became the first centre manager, while throughout

[222] Neil Barklem, 'Three Month Report to Centerprise Collective from Neil Barklem, Administrator and Fundraiser Worker', 18 February 1991, A Hackney Autobiography, Bishopsgate Institute.

[223] Centerprise Trust Ltd, 'Centerprise Annual Report 1991', 1991, A Hackney Autobiography, Bishopsgate Institute.

[224] Centerprise Trust Ltd, 'Centerprise Annual Report 1986'.

[225] Centerprise Trust Ltd, 'Centerprise Annual Report 1992'.

the organisation the collective was replaced with a hierarchical management structure. The Centerprise reports emphasised that the end of the workers' collective was intended to increase the authority and oversight of the Council of Management over the organisation.

For many of the workers this was a difficult period. Dorothea described there being "a lot of mistrust and anxiety around us not being a collective anymore, because, at the time it kind of felt like a divide-and-rule kind of tactic on the part of Hackney Council." Claudia describes her anger that as the collective ended so did parity of pay. She was offered more pay than older and more experienced co-workers. With the move to a conventional management and pay structure the more "manual" jobs were paid less than the administrative or "intellectual" roles, as Claudia describes: "There was a guy that did the caretaking, and his wife cleaned as well. They got the same pay as everybody else. And suddenly they were on £3 an hour, or £4, whatever it was in those days. Whereas before everybody was on £8 an hour, which was a lot then. Suddenly it was like, hang on, you're lesser than us, you're cleaning our shit up, literally, and, because I'm pen-pushing all week, I'm going to be on forty grand, or whatever it was, thirty grand."

Pressure from both outside and within Centerprise brought an end to collective management, but it seems likely that the frustration of many workers with its time-consuming, unsupportive aspects gradually eroded the commitment needed to keep it going. Some, like Dorothea, disliked the way the transition happened more than the actual change. With the end of the collective, she says, came the "relief of autonomy … I didn't have to involve myself in making decisions about the advice centre, which I didn't know anything about." Jean Milloy, who left Centerprise in 1989, after eleven years at Centerprise in a variety of roles reflected: "I think, what happened was that there were staff changes, people were less inclined to maintain the collective idea. And didn't want to be spending part of their week serving in the coffee bar, if what they were there for was to give people advice. I think that's what gradually happened, that the whole collective thing just became too much really. I could see people who felt less committed to it as a way of working, less convinced."

1993 was described in the Chair's Report as a year "of struggle at Centerprise."[226] An internal conflict, centred around accusations of corruption, resulted in the departure of many members of the Council of Management. Neil Barklem was replaced by finance director Emmanuel Amevor, who would continue to manage Centerprise until its closure in 2012. Amidst this turmoil Hackney Council suspended its funding in October 1993, meaning that the staff went without wages for several months. Judith Skinner, who had recently joined Centerprise as bookshop manager describes this as: "an awful financial crisis … We were, you know, on the point of bankruptcy, and we actually had to stop trading for a while because, because there was the possibility that we might have been trading while insolvent or something, which was against the law. So, the bookshop was actually closed for a bit,

[226] Centerprise Trust Ltd, 'Centerprise Annual Report 1993', 1993, A Hackney Autobiography, Bishopsgate Institute.

and we weren't paid, and, and it was terrible. I was terrified, I had a mortgage. It was a very turbulent time."

By 1995, a recovery seems to have been made. That year's report relates that Centerprise was "flourishing and developing in new directions", with an expansion of its youth work and a prestigious new literature development project which continued some of the functions of the, now closed, publishing project.[227] Judith Skinner had got to work increasing the profitability of the shop. She had previously worked at the feminist bookshop and co-operative, Sisterwrite, and also at a Penguin bookshop, where she had gained valuable experience in working in more commercially-oriented bookselling. Judith changed the way the books were displayed and opened the shop earlier in the mornings: "I thought we actually did have to be open before half past ten." The building was no longer closed for Monday meetings, and so the shops were open six days a week. She describes turnover increasing rapidly in her first few years in charge of the bookshop, helped by the acquisition of a computer, meaning they could complete lucrative library orders more easily.

However, despite increased profits in the shops Centerprise remained reliant on grant income, and the financial situation remained precarious, not helped by the abolition in 1997 of the Net Book Agreement, which had protected smaller shops from being undercut by the larger chains' ability to discount books. From the mid-1990s onwards some of the projects at Centerprise slowly began to close or offer a much reduced service run by volunteers. Erita Crawford continued to manage the coffee bar for many years, while the bookshop was run by Emmanuel Amevor, the centre director.

The closure

In its final years Centerprise seemed invincible to some, an institution that could go on forever. Others were surprised it hadn't already shut. The coffee bar remained an important space for community interaction. Pauline Wiltshire says that it was "a place for people who couldn't go anywhere much. It was like a meeting place really, mostly for older people who need somewhere to go, to sit down, have a meal and chit-chat."

Pan-African community activist and educator Toyin Agbetu used Centerprise right up until its closure in 2012. As a child, and science fiction fanatic, Toyin had enjoyed how "Centerprise" sounded like "Enterprise". An early piece of his writing submitted to a local writing competition, *Anansi and the Magic Pot*, won and was displayed at Centerprise. Just a few years before it closed, Toyin used the coffee bar to host informal Sunday afternoon gatherings: "So what I'd do is that I would cycle down to Centerprise ... I'd bring Oware and Scrabble and a deck of cards. I'd sit down in my spot, and read the *Observer* newspaper with a group of people who would pull up chairs. It would get bigger and bigger. And we'd all just talk about the issues that week. And that was very successful. I mean it wasn't meant to be anything

[227] Centerprise Trust Ltd, 'Centerprise Annual Report 1995', 1995, A Hackney Autobiography, Bishopsgate Institute.

other than just people coming together, but it was almost like a surgery."

In 2010 Hackney Council raised Centerprise's historically low rent to its normal charity rate, totalling £37,000 a year for the entire premises. Centerprise offered to pay an increased rent of £12,000 a year but this was rejected by the Council. Eventually a court judgement ordered Centerprise to vacate the premises, pay legal costs and £50,000 in rent arrears.[228] A campaign was organised, but could not prevent the closure. Toyin expresses a sense of disbelief that after forty-two years, Centerprise could close so suddenly:

> It seemed like an institution. I mean people treated it as an institution. It wasn't treated as a commercial building. It was pretty much in the minds of many people that, Centerprise has always been here, it's always going to be here, it's always been serving this role. How could it just vanish? That's just not going to happen, there'll be a last minute reprieve, the political shift to the right couldn't be that mean.

Turning up at Centerprise to celebrate the launch of *Stranger in a Borrowed Land*, a biography of writer Lotte Moos, ex-publishing workers Ken Worpole and Maggie Hewitt found themselves locked out, the shutters were down, and a note on the door said "Closed by the Council." Centerprise had been evicted the preceding Friday, 2 November, 2012.

Pauline Wiltshire felt "bitter" about the closure:

> This is the council for you. They like to take over things, when you have things that you're happy with they decide to change it over into something else, which we're not happy with. Didn't bother ask none of us, you know, "Would you like this to be done," whatever. They just think, "Oh yeah, it's time something else was there."

Judith Skinner reflects that the closure of Centerprise must have been a "huge loss" because "the people that you see now sitting outside the cafés, who probably won't be welcomed inside, they would have been inside Centerprise then." Local resident Pauline Brown echoes this sentiment:

> Coming from the market, where do we go? We're shopping, Centerprise, sit down, we have a meal, we talk. And, we didn't have to know anybody, but we talk with each other. I can only tell you what I see of it, what I can remember of it, that it was a place was holding up the community and, people wasn't walking around, wandering. Centerprise was there, they could go and sit there all day if they want, no one harassed them, attack them, "Get out!" You can talk to people, can communicate. Come out feeling fresh and feeling nice. So, it was a place was holding up Hackney. I'm looking around, but there isn't a place like Centerprise.

---

[228] Syma Mohammed, 'Centerprise Ousted from Property in Kingsland Road Following Legal Wrangle', *Hackney Gazette*, 5 November 2012, http://www.hackneygazette.co.uk/news/centerprise_ousted_from_property_in_kingsland_road_following_legal_wrangle_1_1682295.

Photograph of Ridley Road Market closing for the day, for the publication *Breaking the Silence: Writing by Asian Women*, 1984. Copyright © Anna Sherwin.

6: Conclusion

Hackney now has several local bookshops, an almost endless number of places to buy coffee and scores of art galleries, music venues, cinemas and theatres. Social enterprise, in some ways reminiscent of Centerprise's fusion of community and commerce, "pops up" all over the place. However, the way that the area has changed has left many locals feeling excluded. Local resident and social entrepreneur Oleander Agbetu explains that the changes are: "a massive message to the African-Caribbean community that there's nothing here for us anymore. Because, when you look at all the businesses that are opening dotted around Hackney, there's not very many people that look like us, that actually own those businesses."

All this change is in danger of erasing the memory of the recent past, its struggles, injustices and achievements, as Toyin Agbetu (TA) and Oleander Agbetu (OA) discuss:

TA:

> Sandringham Road, Kingsland Road, it was like a community hub, which now feels like it's been broken. Before this wave of gentrification there was a collective memory of resistance to oppression, resistance to police brutality. I want another word for gentrification, because, what's happened feels like more than just gentrification. I mean that's not –

OA:

> Someone called it social cleansing.

TA:

> That's a bit harsh, but yeah, that kind of social cleansing, and white-washing. It's a rich history that can't be eradicated, because people who grew up in Hackney, still remember it. And as long as we still remember it, it's there, it still exists. All that's happened is it's gone underground.

Legacies of the wave of community activity that began in the early 1970s can still be found in the area's fabric, even if the radical origins of some community facilities now seem obscure. The Hackney Playbus drives up to entertain local children, the Rio Cinema, just across the road from where Centerprise stood, is open for business, having been saved from closure by a community takeover in 1979 and Sandbrook Playgroup in Stoke Newington is one of many childcare facilities set up by the direct action of local parents.[229] Centerprise has disappeared from the high street but its memory is carried by the many people who were part of it, and long after direct memories fade, the extraordinary range of books it published will survive on shelves, in homes and libraries.

Centerprise was always about more than the individual services it

---

[229] See http://hackney-playbus.org/, http://riocinema.org.uk, http://wwwsandbrookplaygroup.co.uk/ and http://www.hackneygazette.co.uk/news/heritage/parent_power_radical_stoke_newington_nursery_sandbrook_is_going_strong_40_years_on_1_462174

offered. It aimed to be a place available to anyone, not just as a place to use, but a place to be part of. They wrote in 1978 that "the conjunction of activities that we try to hold together is a statement about possible futures as well as a permanently unfinished agenda for the present."[230] The hope was that if someone came in for one reason, a cup of tea, some advice, they might leave having discovered a host of other things. Hackney resident Pauline Brown first walked past Centerprise in the 1970s, but didn't venture inside: "Because, you see the market was there, Dalston market, Ridley Road Market, the famous market in England, right? We just used to walk past it all the time. But I did not know what was going on in Centerprise at that time."

Pauline travelled from Jamaica to join her mother in England in the mid-1960s when she was around ten years old. Later, living in Hackney, she worked for a while in the Burberry factory, before becoming a school cook. She first came into Centerprise for advice in the 1980s when her wages had not been paid, and quickly discovered and made use of the bookshop, café, cultural events and reading centre. She continued to visit Centerprise regularly from then on until it closed in 2012. What made Centerprise somewhere Pauline enjoyed spending time was:

> nobody worry your head, nobody bother you, nobody was attacking you. So, we could go in there for long; the canteen was there, sit down, you read books. The books what was there was really giving us something back, we could read about someone's story. There are so many books in there to help us with our ability, and the books in there are so spiritual, the words were so great, so sweet ... Because we are reading about someone else. And then, when you're reading some of these books, I look back into my life and say, well, that's me, that is me.

Pauline describes herself as a creative person and talks about both taking and giving something to places like Centerprise: "I've been to all these places that inspire my life, and when I go to all these places, I look, and observe, I study things. I see what's going on. I see what can come out of it. And I see what I can get out of it, what satisfaction I can get from it. It's not just to go in there. A lot of places inspire me, they inspire me, I inspire those places." Centerprise had a reciprocal relationship with its customers, who created the place as much as they consumed it.

Some people who first came in casually as customers later volunteered, became workers or joined the management committee. Neil Martinson, one of the original group of "intellectual unclubbable" school students who frequented Centerprise, was twenty-two when he joined the collective as a publishing worker. Centerprise, he says, was like his university: "I think it didn't so much open up doors, but just open up different ways of thinking really." Neil reflects that his involvement with Centerprise profoundly changed the course of his life. As a rebellious young man, frustrated by class inequality and injustice, he had walked out of school without taking his exams.

[230] Centerprise Trust Ltd, 'Centerprise Annual Report 1978.'

Conclusion

Barbara Schulz, 1982. Photograph courtesy of Wendy Pettifer.

Centerprise not only gave him a job, he says it provided an outlet for his anger "in a much more constructive way". At the publishing project, he managed complex projects and learnt a lot from the people he worked alongside. For others, Centerprise provided a "safe haven." Barbara Schulz first came to Centerprise in the 1980s. She was fourteen and was bunking off school with her friends:

> It was somewhere that we felt was quite safe, it was a coffee bar, we could sit there, they didn't throw people out, we didn't have to spend lots of money. And we just liked the feel of the place, it was different to what we had usually seen around Hackney. And people were friendly and respectful towards us, they weren't, you know, oh god, kids, get out of here. So, that was quite attractive.

Barbara says she "grew up from" Centerprise during a difficult time in her life, as she came out as a lesbian, ran away from home and left school:

I was insecure, really nervous. I stuttered a lot. I don't know how I managed to get it together to run away [from home], but I did, it was like, the big step. But, I think, being at Centerprise, it made me feel secure, more confident in myself to go out and do things. So, actually it made me realise, I don't have to put up with the bully, I don't have to live in these circumstances, I can do it for myself, I will do it for myself. It gave me that sort of strength, the young people and the people there. And, the whole thing about education, it stimulated me to push myself.

Apart from spending a lot of time hanging out at Centerprise Barbara joined the Hackney Girls Project, and later got involved in the Centerprise Young Photographers' Group and Hackney Unemployed Media Scheme. Soon she was helping the youth workers to run these groups and developed a passion for photography. She got a Saturday job at Centerprise, starting off washing up in the café and later becoming a sessional youth worker. Her involvement had grown to the extent that "after a while it wasn't a haven, it was just somewhere that I was part of." Barbara maintained a strong connection with Centerprise until the early 1990s, when changes there and in her own life meant she was ready to move on. By then she had a child of her own and was becoming a qualified youth worker. She later gained a Cultural Studies degree, and became a teacher.

Centerprise helped Barbara push herself, partly because, she says, she felt a sense of inequality with the university educated people she met there. She explains that: "I think by being involved in the Young Writers project, I was getting into doing things, and writing, and feeling that I needed to gain more skills, and I didn't want to be this person that didn't have any qualifications. So, although I was feeling more confident in myself I felt stupid, I felt I hadn't got the relevant qualifications to be an equal." Roger Mills also thinks that one of the educational aspects of Centerprise for him was how it brought people with different experiences of education together: "Again, it's to do with this sort of, slightly class issue that some of the people there were university educated, so they'd have a different fix on things and different way of operating. So, I think Centerprise did definitely act as a sort of educational thing. I didn't go to university, but I went to Centerprise. So, perhaps that filled that gap."

The mixture of people involved in Centerprise was educational for all involved. Claudia Manchanda, for instance, describes how much she learnt from her colleague Erita Crawford, when they ran the coffee bar together. Claudia was only nineteen when she started working at Centerprise, and Erita was in her fifties:

"She had been working there for quite a number of years, and she was a great charismatic character. And, she taught me a lot about just having humility as a person, and how to treat people in life. She was like a sort of role model of how to treat people. And she was quite a devout Christian, but sort of shattered all my illusions of Christianity. She was genuinely a loving person, completely un-homophobic, completely open, completely caring. And had really clear boundaries, which I needed as a teenager as well. She used to tell me off if I was late, and I learnt how to sort of behave as a proper person in that job."

Many describe working at Centerprise as a "privilege". Jean Milloy says "It was a brave attempt to find a different way of working. And I think it did good for a lot of people, including the workers, or some of them anyway." Irene Schwab is proud to have been part of something so "important and exciting" despite "all the difficulties and responsibilities and the worries." Experience gained at Centerprise was used by many workers in their subsequent careers, some continuing to teach in adult education, work in advice or publishing, others going on to work in academia, others as artists, screenwriters, poets, and some as managers in local government or the NHS. Poet and former black arts worker Dorothea Smartt reflects that "at that time in my own personal, creative development, there were things that I needed as an artist, as a writer, and because I was at Centerprise I was able to make those things happen, not just for me, but for anyone else who wanted to come along to them as well." Academic and former reading centre tutor Liesbeth de Block says "it gave me skills, an awareness of starting from where people are, rather than coming in and imposing what should happen." She ponders that "Centerprise gave me a better sense of education as part of wider community."

Centerprise could not be everything to everyone but the unique combination of activities found behind the shopfronts, combined with its ability to welcome and serve an incredibly diverse range of people and involve a smaller number in its inner workings, held open doors to many that may otherwise have remained firmly shut. Jud Stone says she thought it was "worthwhile because people were really trying to do something, to make things good for themselves and other people and enjoy it. We were trying to make a community and to share skills, share expertise, build things, rather than knocking them down."

Following spread: **Centerprise after it closed, 2013. © Alan Denney.**

The Lime Green Mystery

Conclusion